REVIVING THE
FINANCIALLY DISTRESSED
BUSINESS

REVIVING THE
FINANCIALLY DISTRESSED
BUSINESS

COMPILED AND EDITED BY

BRIAN L. DAVIDOFF

CONTRIBUTING AUTHORS

SAMUEL R. BIGGS · STEPHEN J. DONELL
LAWRENCE N. HURWITZ · HOWARD B. GROBSTEIN
HENRY KASKOV · CHUCK KLAUS
JEFFREY A. KRIEGER · MARK LEFKO
C. JOHN M. MELISSINOS · NEVIN SANLI
JOEL B. WEINBERG

EMPORION PRESS

Published by EMPORION PRESS 2019

A division of Antaeus Books

Copyright © 2018 by Greenberg Glusker Fields Claman & Machtinger LLP

ISBN: 978-0-578-42786-7 (Paperback)

ISBN: 978-0-578-44723-0 (Ebook)

Library of Congress Control Number: 2019931044

Cover illustration: Michael Rohani

Book design by DesignForBooks.com

Printed in the U.S.A.

Contents

5 Turnaround Accounting
BY SAMUEL R. BIGGS

6 Debt Financing for the Insolvent Company
LAWRENCE N. HURWITZ

8 Sale Transactions

Introduction

O ver the course of the last 35 years, I have had the privilege of working with many talented business owners and senior-level management whose companies, for one reason or another, have been beset with financial difficulty. No one sets out in business to fail, but despite our best efforts, this sometimes occurs. The reasons are multiple and varied: Sometimes there is a change in the industry and the business has not been able to evolve to meet the changing marketplace (think records, 8-track tapes, CDs, MP3s, DVDs, and, now, streaming music). Sometimes it is the pressure of increased competition and reduced prices (think TVs). Other times it could be that a significant customer fails to pay, causing a negative chain reaction or an adverse judgement. More often than not, what I see in entrepreneur-operated businesses is that the business owner is skilled at the core business of the company, whether that is selling watermelons or manufacturing widgets, but is less skilled or focused on the "back office" operations. This too often results in inadequate record keeping and improper financial and operational information being provided to the owners/operators, as a result of which bad decisions are made. For whatever reason you find your business at the crossroads of financial distress, this book can be your guide to finding your way through the morass.

Over the years during which I have counseled so many clients back to financial health, I have collaborated with a variety of business professionals whose skills I have called on to help my clients with the many specialized needs that arise in this complex intersection of finance, accounting, and law. It occurred to me that is a dearth of resources for the business owner to find in one place the voices of the professionals who come together to help restructure businesses.

Within these pages, you will hear from experienced professionals who have assisted financially distressed companies in many different industries with restructurings, reorganizations, asset sales, mergers and acquisitions, workouts, and liquidations, whether out of court or through formal bankruptcy cases. Their experiences, observations, and stories lend insight into how others have addressed these stressful circumstances and provide alternative strategies for correcting the course, while yielding some peace of mind.

I practice law in Southern California, and the advisers who share their thoughts in this book also hail from Southern California. However, the topics that are raised and the issues that are dealt with in this book are germane to any distressed business no matter where located in the United States.

Through these pages we will illuminate what lies ahead for the financially distressed business and guide you toward the best possible solution for you and your company. Financial restructuring is a complex topic with a host of technical and legal terms and jargon. This book is designed to be accessible to the business owner and address the issues from a business perspective. Neither the length nor the tenor of this book is intended to be an in-depth study of the many topics covered. It will, however, provide the reader an excellent overview of both the challenges of, and opportunities available in, a distressed business restructuring process.

My thanks go out to my fellow practitioners in the restructuring world who have taken their time to record their thoughts and observations, in each case with the benefit of multiple years of experience. Two of those practitioners are my law partners, Jeff Krieger and John Melissinos, with whom I have had the privilege of working at our law firm Greenberg Glusker LLP in Los Angeles, and who bring their own special skills to our legal practice and to this book.

Brian L. Davidoff
Editor

1

Managing the Financially Distressed Business

By Brian L. Davidoff

Despite Henry Ford's legacy as an influential innovator and entrepreneur of the late 19th and early 20th centuries, he was no stranger to debt *and* bankruptcy.

Starting out in 1899 with the financial backing of several prominent individuals, the Detroit Automobile Company was established—facing stiff competition from some 60 other aspiring automakers at the time. While the talented young engineer obsessed over the mechanics of his vehicles, the company's productivity suffered, and by mid-1900 the company began its financial collapse. The Detroit Automobile Company produced only 20 cars until the enterprise went bankrupt in 1901.

Undeterred, later that year Ford reorganized into the Henry Ford Company, again with the help of investors. As the story goes, this time he failed to brand and market his vehicles properly—the public did not quite understand Ford's invention—sales floundered and the company dissolved shortly after.

When his second company proved unsuccessful, he put all of his hopes into a make-or-break third effort. In June 1903,

The Ford Motor Company, with the help of investor Alexander Malcomson, rolled out its first car, the Model A, and the rest is history.

— ◇ —

For the countless businesses struggling to cope with obstacles—reduced demand, increased competition, scarcity of capital, changing business models, etc.—reshaping strategy is critical to surviving and prospering in today's economy. Indeed, unforeseen events out of the business owners' control inevitably occur, but how business owners react to and plan for such events can significantly impact their ability to survive, and thrive. At the first signs of distress, survivors commit to proactive management and rely upon the guidance of professional counselors.

Warning Signs

Financial problems often arise when the business owner is busy focusing on sales and building the business, while ignoring the red flags that signal instability. Although any number of factors can cause weakness, it is often that the business owner does not receive adequate financial information that reflects true performance. Or, the owner may have credible data but does not pay sufficiently close attention or take the time to understand what that information means to the business, thus missing the warning signs.

One thing I've seen time and time again is that owners of "survivor companies" all face their challenges early and earnestly. Doing so provides more options and makes the process less painful. On the other hand, business owners who adopt a "head in the sand" approach, failing to recognize the urgency of financial distress or their responsibility in addressing it, often end up closing their doors.

Astute business owners are always on the lookout for warning signs of financial constraint. They are intimately aware of the status of accounts payable and accounts receivable, their financial statements, and their actual-to-budgeted performance, as well as how they are trending. With this knowledge, they can often preempt devastating events through managing the expectations of banks, creditors, employees, and others. Those who wait too long to address shortfalls face potentially dire consequences, such as:

- a call from the bank alerting management that financial ratios or loan covenants under its credit agreement are out of compliance;

- notice of a lawsuit or a "writ of attachment" from a creditor or vendor seeking to freeze assets pending the outcome of a trial;

- significant or sudden turnover of management staff, due to the personal stress that accompanies poor business performance and causes them to move on to greener pastures;

- the unwillingness of vendors to provide further trade credit; or

- the "set-off" or freezing of the business's bank account due to loan delinquency.

If the business has gotten to the point that the bank account is frozen, this is a sure sign that management has waited too long and, unfortunately, will have limited options going forward. For example, the prospect of moving away from the existing bank lender to a more flexible asset-based lender or accounts receivable finance lender will be much more difficult in the face of an attachment, or with negative cash flow.

Early Action

One cannot overemphasize the advantage of addressing a company's financial problems early and swiftly. Early action by the business owner will often temper or eliminate the worst consequences.

For example, when a sign manufacturer first realized his business was in trouble, he immediately engaged a bankruptcy attorney and a turnaround consultant to help him work through his issues. The turnaround team was able to pacify the bank, get the books and records in order, and appease his vendors and creditors. The business owner's early action in handing off the legal issues and dealings with the bank and creditors to professionals experienced in dealing with these matters allowed him to focus exclusively on his business operations. Of course, many other factors contributed to the successful restructuring of his company, but at a time when the company's operations needed the owner's considerable attention, the decision to hand off specific responsibilities helped put his business back on track. After the turnaround, he was able to sell his business and pay off his guaranteed debt.

In this case, had the owner not acted when he did, the business may have continued its downward slide leading to eventual liquidation, leaving the owner nothing in the end except bad credit, and possibly regret.

In another example of early action, a company engaged restructuring professionals at the onset of a litigation matter that, if adversely decided, would have resulted in the seizure of the company's assets. The company, working together with those key professionals, developed an advance plan to continue operations if the litigation result were adverse. But the litigation resolved favorably and, because the business owner understood the importance of preemptive planning, the company is still in business today.

When to Hire a Consultant

It is not surprising and is indeed understandable that the business owner will usually defer, for as long as possible, the cost of hiring outside professionals. However, never has the adage of "an ounce of prevention is worth a pound of cure" been truer. For the survival of a financially distressed business, the best time to hire a professional turnaround consultant is now!

Financial pressure often plays a significant role in delaying the engagement of professionals. If the company can barely pay its way, how can it afford the additional cost of outside professionals? Counter-intuitively, the opposite is true. The cost to deal with the more moderate issues in the early stages of financial distress is often far less than the price of the same professionals when deep in the throes of a crisis. More often than not, the length of the professionals' engagement with the company will be much shorter, less intense, and more productive when engaged early.

Far too often business owners are reticent to hire a consultant or attorney because they think that they know their businesses best and believe that they are most capable of directing them during their critical hours. While part of that thinking may be true—they certainly know their businesses—if they have never have managed a company in financial distress, they will quickly learn that an entirely different skill set and specialized experience are required.

For one, the turnaround consultant can pinpoint the exact issues to address. While expertise in a particular business line is helpful, it is the consultant's understanding of the mechanics and dynamics of financial distress—how it affects not only the balance sheet of the company but the psyche of its creditors— that is important. Even more important is having someone on the team who knows how to address those effects.

For example, when a business carries inventory, a turn-around consultant will determine whether the books overstate that inventory, a common problem with financially distressed companies and one that management is not accustomed to reviewing. In the many distressed company cases in which I have been involved when one of the business assets was inventory, it was, indeed, the rare occasion that inventory was not overstated on the company's books. Although not usually a focal point of the business owner, this nevertheless is critical to address in order to correct the company's financial woes. Similarly, too often the business owner believes that building up additional inventory is a viable way to collateralize a lender. The opposite, however, is typically true. Excess inventory uses cash, which is so precious to a struggling company.

A consultant will also have considerably more experience in approaching a bank whose loan may be in default. He or she will understand the mindset of the creditors who may be clamoring for payment and the employees who are likely nervous about losing their jobs. Handing off these details to a consultant will allow management to continue to focus on the business itself.

Whether justified or not, when a company is past due with its vendors and other creditors, blame will be placed on management. The creditors will also typically be more cautious in dealing with management and regard them as less credible. Another significant contribution of a qualified turnaround consultant is the credibility that he or she can bring to the business's creditors, who may have lost confidence in the company's management team. As an objective third party, the turnaround consultant may be able to persuade vendors to continue to supply product on credit, or may even successfully negotiate additional financing from the company's bank. For example, a bank will typically move a defaulted loan from the regular loan officer to a "special assets" officer, who is accustomed to working with turnaround consultants. In cases in which the owner is not already working with a specialist, the bank officer will probably recommend a turnaround consultant to the business owner anyway.

Finally, having an experienced turnaround consultant on board at the onset is particularly valuable if the business ultimately has to file bankruptcy. Since the consultant has expertise in the bankruptcy court process, he or she can anticipate the procedural issues that may arise. The consultant can "talk the language" of bankruptcy with attorneys and creditors and can prepare the many necessary financial documents for and during a bankruptcy filing.

Candor as an Ally

When a business becomes financially distressed, an owner's first reaction may be to "keep it under wraps." The owner may withhold information to the company's bank, creditors, and employees. Unfortunately, that tactic is rarely, if ever, helpful. The reality is that everything will inevitably be exposed. It is far better for the owner to be in control of how and when that happens. If a lender, creditor, or key employee learns about untoward business events from third parties, rather than directly from the source, creditors and lenders tend to lose confidence in their borrowers, and key employees lose valuable trust.

The way one communicates information to stakeholders is crucial. If vendors and creditors have been calling without returned calls, their natural tendency is to think the worst. Getting back to them with a response is vital to the outcome. And this is where a turnaround consultant can be particularly helpful. He or she can lend credibility and promote a level of confidence by establishing discreet contact promptly, as well as build rapport with suppliers, creditors, and lenders—essential relationships in a turnaround.

When ownership is forthright in dealing with its lender regarding the financial problems of its business, the bank is more likely to work with owners and permit the business to keep operating. To the extent that the bank believes the owner is straightforward and that the business can succeed, a bank is more likely to give such accommodations. In some cases, banks are known to help the owner reorganize, sell the business, or even find a new lender, provided that the borrower has been forthcoming in the initial disclosure of the issues and that the lender is kept informed as the turnaround proceeds.

Likewise, it is tactically necessary to determine which employees and managers "need to know." Being candid and upfront helps engender support from employees, as opposed to allowing them to dwell on the fear of the unknown. Therefore, enlisting employee support in the turnaround process is essential. Letting employees know that professional help is engaged and that the turnaround program is underway may prevent employee attrition and production fall-off.

Undoubtedly, in a competitive market, one needs to be careful of allowing customers or competitors to learn of financial distress. A business must balance being forthright with those stakeholders who need to know and the information that is allowed to permeate into the marketplace. This strategy should be addressed early on in the restructuring process.

The Downside of Not Being Forthright

A business that rented durable medical devices, such as wheelchairs that patients needed on a long-term basis, engaged my law firm when it became apparent that the owner was having financial difficulties. Unfortunately, the owner refused to acknowledge that *any* problems were attributable to his management. He viewed all of the issues as being caused by someone else—the bank would not lend enough, the sales people were not bringing in enough sales, etc. Even though, at our urging, he hired a team of turnaround professionals to help him with the situation, he would not give the team members authority to do what they needed to do or to disclose necessary information to creditors and lenders. Primarily as a result of his approach, when the company filed for bankruptcy, the consultants were unable to implement the required changes. Furthermore, the bankruptcy judge felt that the company had not provided accurate information. In his dealings, the owner also had accrued little credibility with the lender and creditors, which eventually forced the chapter 11 reorganization into a chapter 7 liquidation.

If the business owner had allowed the team to do what they had been hired to do, the business could have been sold (there was a buyer in the wings) rather than liquidated. Later, the business owner also had to file personal bankruptcy because he had personally guaranteed the bank debt.

The Upside of Full Disclosure

In another example, we represented the owner of a food distribution business who engaged us early in the process, and we brought on a turnaround consultant. We worked together as a team, bringing together management and financial and legal expertise. The company ultimately filed bankruptcy because of its unresolved financial problems. But in this case, the company *was* able to reorganize, pay much of what it owed to its creditors, and continue to stay in business. Because the business owner understood the need for addressing the issues early, openly, and honestly, with full disclosure, the team was successful. The creditors recognized that they were dealing with honest and accountable management, and were willing to work with the company to give it an opportunity to correct its problems.

Building Your Turnaround Team

When a business is in a difficult financial situation, and the owner recognizes the need to hire professionals to help, where do you start? First, call your accountant or regular attorney.

The attorney. In most cases, not just any attorney will do. You will want one who specializes in business restructuring; not a personal bankruptcy attorney or a general business attorney. Experience with business bankruptcy laws and other turnaround techniques is essential. If you do not know someone like this, you may be able to get a referral from your regular attorney or accountant.

Consulting the American Bankruptcy Institute (abi.org) is a good start. The ABI is the nation's most significant association of bankruptcy professionals, made up of over 12,000 members in multidisciplinary roles, including attorneys, auctioneers, bankers, judges, lenders, professors, turnaround specialists, accountants, and others. An ABI-Certified Business Bankruptcy attorney is usually a good choice. This designation requires that a specific portion of the attorney's practice is in the business bankruptcy area and that he or she takes continuing legal education to be recertified on a regular basis. Several other professional organizations, such as the Turnaround Management Association, also have highly capable members who specialize in this area. Most importantly, the attorney must be a member of the state bar in the state in which the attorney practices and, more specifically, the attorney should also be a member of the section of the state bar which focuses on bankruptcy.

Additionally, there is great benefit in hiring an attorney who has been in the community in which the business is located and has experience with turnaround situations. Such an attorney will likely know some of the other lawyers, accountants, appraisers, and professionals who will be involved in the process. In addition to your attorney, an attorney will represent the bank, another might represent unsecured creditors, and others will represent various interested parties in the restructuring. If the attorney you choose is known and respected by his or her peers, the attorney will have additional credibility, which can enable you to accomplish more in a shorter period.

The turnaround consultant. Another member of the team who could have a decisive impact on your success is the turnaround consultant. Some turnaround specialists work within large national firms, while others are solo practitioners. If your attorney or accountant does not make a recommendation, ensure that the consultant you engage is a Certified Insolvency Reorganization Advisor. The CIRA designation is usually a sign of significant experience, something you do not want to sacrifice.

The public relations consultant. Generally speaking, although more critical for a large company, a well-known brand, or when public perception is key, a business should consider involving a public relations consultant who deals with crisis management. Again, a recommendation from one of your existing advisors is probably the best approach to choosing appropriately.

Other Professionals. Other professionals whom a company may need to engage include an appraiser, if the valuation of the business is a part of the restructuring program; a liquidator, if the sale of excess assets is necessary; an accountant, if the books and records are in shambles; or an investment banker, if a sale of the company is part of the restructuring plan.

When Bankruptcy is the Only Option

In other chapters of this book, we will discuss several different turnaround options apart from formal bankruptcy proceedings. If, however, bankruptcy is determined to be your only option, three types are relevant to the business owner: chapter 7 liquidation, chapter 11 reorganization, or chapter 13 individual repayment programs. While chapter 7 and 11 filings usually are voluntary (i.e., the company makes an affirmative decision to file), they can also be involuntary and forced upon a business that is delinquent in payment of its creditors.

Chapter 7. A business should only consider a chapter 7 liquidation if the company is going to cease to operate. The purpose of filing a chapter 7 is to wind up a business and put the liquidation of the assets into the hands of a bankruptcy trustee.

Upon the filing of a chapter 7, a chapter 7 trustee is appointed by the Office of the United States Trustee. The Office of the United States Trustee is a branch of the U.S. Department of Justice, whose role is to monitor bankruptcy cases and to appoint chapter 7 trustees. Each jurisdiction in the United States has a panel of chapter 7 trustees, who are selected by the Office of the United States Trustee. The chapter 7 trustees are often lawyers or accountants whose practices include acting as chapter 7 trustees.

Once the chapter 7 is filed, the debtor is required to attend a meeting of creditors, which usually occurs between four and six weeks after the filing of the bankruptcy case. The debtor company is also required to cooperate with the trustee and provide to the trustee the books and records of the business as requested by the trustee.

The principal benefit of chapter 7 liquidation is the finality it brings to the cessation of the business. A notice is sent to creditors by the bankruptcy court indicating both that the company has filed a chapter 7 bankruptcy and whether assets are available for distribution.

It is significant to note that for an entity (non-individual) debtor, a chapter 7 does *not* discharge the debts of the company. However, the notice that is sent by the bankruptcy court indicating that the company has ceased business and is liquidating in a chapter 7 usually causes creditors to acknowledge the inability to collect their claims. Even so, because there is no legal discharge after the conclusion of the bankruptcy case, legally the company still owes the debt. Accordingly, one should never use the entity that has gone through the chapter 7 for whatever new business the owner may seek to start.

If assets are available for distribution, creditors may file claims in the bankruptcy case and receive a pro rata distribution of the available assets. This notice also allows the directors and officers of a company to "close the books" of the company after concluding its chapter 7.

The benefit of a chapter 7 bankruptcy is that a chapter 7 trustee is assigned to take control of the assets and is responsible for conducting the liquidation and disposal of the assets. This is important if the company either has no remaining management or does not have finances available to hire somebody to conduct the winding down of the business.

A chapter 7 is usually not a viable method of maintaining the going-concern value of a business. Chapter 7 is designed for liquidation, and it is only in rare circumstances that the chapter 7 trustee will request the court for authority to operate the business before selling the assets. Even if the intention *is* to liquidate the company's assets through a chapter 7, chapter 7 is usually not the preferable route for causing a quick disposition of the assets, possibly to an identified buyer. This is because chapter 7 trustees often handle many cases, and it is often difficult to get the attention of the trustee at the outset of the case to engage in a quick sale of the assets. Accordingly, chapter 7 is often relegated to those cases in which the business owner is ready to walk away from the business and hand over the job of disposing of the assets to a third party under court supervision.

One final word of caution: it is part of the job of the chapter 7 trustee to investigate the financial affairs of the debtor company. This may include the trustee's evaluating whether there are any so-called "avoidance actions"—preferences and avoidable transfer actions-that may be brought against either creditors of the company or the management. (See below for a discussion of avoidance actions.) Accordingly, if there is concern that such an action may be brought against the principals of the company, there should be careful analysis before any such bankruptcy filing. Any good bankruptcy attorney would ordinary complete such an analysis before recommending the filing of a chapter 7 bankruptcy.

Chapter 11. Unlike the objective of liquidation of a chapter 7, a chapter 11 is designed to reorganize a business. The management of the business typically remains in place and becomes a debtor in possession, or DIP, in the chapter 11 bankruptcy. No trustee is appointed unless the DIP has engaged in inappropriate conduct or other fraudulent acts, in which event a trustee might be appointed.

Chapter 11 is very flexible. It allows a company to liquidate under the control of the DIP, sell the assets, or reorganize. More often than not, management (often with professional assistance) is in a better position than a trustee to maximize the return on the asset liquidation or reorganization. The chapter 11 process does, however, require that existing management is available or that funding is available to hire appropriate expert personnel to manage the company through the chapter 11.

Worth noting, the out-of-pocket cost to the lender and/or investor of a chapter 11 bankruptcy tends to be significantly more expensive than in chapter 7. This additional cost, however, is often justified by obtaining a higher return than that from an asset sale or liquidation under the control of management.

Chapter 13. A chapter 13 bankruptcy is a repayment plan for *individuals* who have a regular income. This option is only available to unincorporated businesses. Corporations and limited liability companies—the most common form of businesses—are not eligible to file for this type of bankruptcy.

A chapter 13 is not available if unsecured debts exceed $394,725 or secured debts are less than $1,184,200. (These criteria are in effect in 2017 and valid through 2019. The amounts rise with inflation.)

A chapter 13 trustee is always appointed to distribute the payments to creditors under the chapter 13 payment plan, which must be filed by the debtor. The payment plan requires creditors to be paid over a five-year period out of all excess income over and above permissible expenses.

Reasons for Chapter 11

Chapter 11 is a business reorganization. Its purpose is to allow a financially distressed business a breathing spell, and an opportunity to modify its financial structure. The reasons for filing a chapter 11 are many. Among the most common are

- The company cannot pay its debts.

- Creditors file lawsuits against the business. (Chapter 11 provides a broadly interpreted stay of litigation against the company that pauses any potential action against the company prior to the bankruptcy filing. With limited exceptions, it stays all proceedings, giving the business a breather.)

- A secured creditor seeks to foreclose. (The automatic stay also applies. Say, for example, that the business lender has filed a lawsuit and is preparing to seize the company's bank account to satisfy a part of the debt. Or, for example, that the company has real estate, and the real estate lender is proceeding with a foreclosure. The filing of chapter 11 will cause a stay of any of the above actions.)

- A company is involved in multiple product-liability lawsuits and needs a way to coordinate litigation.

- A company needs to terminate a lease agreement. (For example, when several retail locations are not prospering and the company wants to walk away from leases, the landlords will likely sue the business. Such damages could put the company out of business. However, if the company files bankruptcy, there is the ability to reject a lease agreement, in which case, the landlord's damages become part of the creditors' unsecured claims in the bankruptcy case.)

The Basics of Chapter 11

A separate estate, referred to as the bankruptcy estate, is created upon filing a petition in court for chapter 11 bankruptcy. The business's books and records must clearly separate the pre-petition assets and liabilities from the post-petition assets and liabilities. As discussed below, all actions seeking to recover on pre-petition liabilities are stayed.

In most chapter 11 cases, a creditors' committee is appointed. Three to seven of the most substantial unsecured creditors of the company usually comprise the committee. Its role is to monitor the operations of the chapter 11 company and to have a meaningful say in the ultimate restructuring of the company. The company's management is expected to keep the committee closely involved in the decisions that the company makes. On occasion, when the company and the committee disagree, such matters are resolved by the court.

If the chapter 11 company has a pre-existing secured loan, then bankruptcy law requires that the lender either consents to or the court approves of the use of "cash collateral." By definition, cash collateral is the proceeds generated from the security held by the lender. For example, rents created by real estate security held by a lender are cash collateral. Or, receivables generated from inventory security held by a lender are cash collateral.

In addition to the use of cash collateral, in preparation for a chapter 11 the attorney and turnaround consultant will typically evaluate the need for and availability of chapter 11 financing, called DIP, or debtor in possession, financing, which requires court approval.

As many businesses need additional financing to make it through the chapter 11, the company's existing lender may provide this DIP financing, but only if the lender is satisfied that it will resolve the company's problems and hasten its exit from chapter 11. The turnaround consultant and the attorney are usually integrally involved in helping the company make its case to the lender.

A bankruptcy filing under chapter 11 creates an automatic stay, precluding creditors from pursuing the company's assets. However, not all creditors are "stayed" indefinitely. For example, secured creditors can seek relief from stay by asking the court to allow them "for cause" to pursue their pre-bankruptcy remedies. The court will evaluate the cause on a case-by-case basis by balancing the needs of the company that has filed bankruptcy with the stay's impact on the creditor.

A typical chapter 11 filing for an entrepreneur-operated company can take as little as four months, if the company has done a good job in talking to stakeholders before the filing to get them on board, or as long as two years, if, for example, there is ongoing litigation or other unresolved issues. At any rate, during the bankruptcy case, the business must start showing progress in the reorganization and turnaround. Even though a chapter 11 can provide a "legal cocoon" around the business to allow time to reorganize, ultimately the company must develop a fiscally viable means to restructure.

Plan of Reorganization

The primary objective of chapter 11 is to reorganize, either through a plan of reorganization or by selling the assets. If the court approves the plan of reorganization, it essentially becomes a binding contract for both the bankrupt company and all of its creditors, and it will supersede the prior relationship between the company and its creditors to the extent provided for in the plan. Reorganization plans always divide creditors into various classes, which follow an order of priority. Secured creditors are first, followed by priority creditors, unsecured creditors, and, at the bottom, equity. All creditors within a class must receive the same treatment.

Commonly, secured creditors are entitled to get paid in full, up to the value of their collateral, or to recover their collateral, while unsecured creditors get partial payments, with all treated the same way.

For example, if the plan calls for the unsecured creditors to get 50 cents on the dollar in monthly payments over a two-year period, they must all be given the same terms, unless the company can offer a good reason to the bankruptcy court for different treatment. The payment calculation to unsecured creditors is often the result of negotiation with the creditors' committee, which takes into account how much the company can reasonably be expected to set aside in the future to pay creditors after paying expenses for operations.

The bankruptcy code has a priority scheme for the payout of creditors:

1. Secured Creditors
2. Administrative Creditors (which include the cost of the bankruptcy, wages, taxes, and deposits on goods not delivered, among other items)
3. Unsecured Creditors
4. Equity Holders

In a smaller company, equity owners can continue to own the business after the chapter 11 plan of reorganization is approved by the court. However, there is a rule called the "absolute priority rule." Absolute priority provides that unsecured creditors must be paid in full before equity holders can participate and retain their ownership of the company.

As a practical matter, the creditors of a smaller company are usually not interested in operating that company, and if they stand any hope of seeing recovery after the chapter 11, it will be because the current owners continue to own and operate the company after bankruptcy. Because unsecured creditors are rarely paid 100 percent on the dollar, there is typically a negotiation between the management and creditors during which the creditors will often use the absolute priority rule as leverage to ensure that the company pays the most possible, within reason, in exchange for an agreement to allow the equity owners to retain their ownership.

If creditors do not elect to negotiate with the company owners on a plan and choose to exercise their absolute priority rule rights, then the owners have the right to contribute "new value" to the company (i.e., new money) and repurchase their shares, which are otherwise cancelled in the bankruptcy. The amount of new value that must be paid in to acquire the post-chapter 11 equity ownership will depend on the case and the value of the company at the time of plan confirmation.

Section 363 Sale

Although dealt with in greater detail in chapter 8 of this book, no discussion of chapter 11 bankruptcy would be complete without some discussion of a "363 sale." When a company is not likely to survive a restructuring, its assets may have value to a third-party buyer. Absent legal protection, a buyer of a financially distressed business will usually be concerned that the company's creditors could pursue the acquired business on various legal theories, including "successor liability," and on that basis may decline to purchase assets of such a business.

It is possible that a sale through a chapter 11 bankruptcy can offer the buyer a means to acquire the assets without concern that a creditor of the seller will pursue the buyer, which also enables a way for the creditors to maximize the value of the assets, rather than merely liquidating the company. Such a transaction is known as a "section 363 sale," as the process takes place under section 363 of the U.S. Bankruptcy Code.

In a section 363 sale, the assets that may be subject to bank and other judgment liens can be sold free and clear so that the buyer receives the assets lien free. The cash proceeds for the assets then attach to the liens in the same order and priority as they previously attached to the assets. This process allows the assets to be sold for the maximum price, leaving the disputing parties in the chapter 11 to litigate over the cash paid.

From a buyer's perspective, one of the principal drawbacks of a section 363 sale is that it is subject to overbidding. While it is, theoretically, in the best interests of the bankrupt debtor company, it does expose the buyer to the risk of overbidding and loss of the transaction.

Nonetheless, various devices can be employed by buyers to minimize this possibility. One such way is that a buyer can be designated a "stalking horse," or lead buyer, and enter into a purchase and sale agreement which will have certain protections for the stalking horse that are approved by the bankruptcy court in the event that the stalking horse is not the winning buyer. Other parties usually have the right to overbid the price of the stalking horse at the sale hearing. If they do, the stalking-horse bidder will usually be entitled to a breakup fee, which includes its costs and expenses to investigate and document the agreement.

See also chapter 9 of this book for more detail on assignments.

KEY TAKEAWAYS

Be alert. Watch the financial metrics of the company so that you do not find yourself unaware of the direction the business is heading on the eve of disaster.

Be proactive. Do not wait until the last minute before running out of cash or being shut out of the business premises. Statistically, companies that are proactive in addressing their financial problems have the highest likelihood of surviving.

Be forthcoming. Owners of a financially distressed business who are honest and forthcoming with the people who need to know about the situation, as well as with those who can help, usually get better results. Be transparent with lenders, vendors, shareholders, some or all employees, and the team of people hired to help.

Be savvy. Make sure you ask your attorney and turnaround advisor for all available alternatives.

Be open. Too often business owners cannot accept that their companies are in financial distress and expect—unreasonably—that by continuing what they have done in the past will resolve the situation. Be open to professional advice, including the possibility that you may need to change "the way things have always been done."

Avoidance-Power Actions

No discussion of restructuring alternatives would be complete without mentioning certain "avoidance powers" that a bankruptcy trustee or an assignee has. An avoidance power refers to the right that exists in a bankruptcy case, or an assignment for benefit of creditors (see chapter 9), to "avoid or 'claw' back certain payments" prior to the onset of bankruptcy or the assignment. The idea behind these clawback rights is to enable the bankruptcy trustee or assignee to recover these payments and redistribute them, so that all creditors are treated fairly and no single creditor receives any undue preference in the period leading up to a bankruptcy or assignment.

Preferences

Elements of a Preference. Preference litigation plays an integral role in many bankruptcy cases, whether liquidation or reorganization. Under the bankruptcy code, there are several elements to a preference. A transfer, broadly defined as "every mode, direct or indirect, absolute or conditional, voluntary or involuntary of disposing of or parting with property," must be

- of an interest of the debtor in property—meaning that the property sought to be recovered as a preference must be owned by the debtor and not a third person, for example, property in an escrow for the benefit of a third party;

- to or for the benefit of a creditor—one who has a claim against the debtor (for example, a payment cannot be a preference if prior to the time of the payment the recipient was not already a creditor of the debtor);

- for or on account of an antecedent debt—to be vulnerable, the transfer must constitute the payment of a pre-existing indebtedness (in other words, a payment for a current bill is not a preference);

- made while the debtor was insolvent—basically a balance sheet test, meaning that a debtor is insolvent if its liabilities exceed its assets, and is presumed to have been insolvent during the 90 days immediately preceding the date of bankruptcy;

- on or within 90 days before bankruptcy, or one year for "insiders," such as officers, directors, shareholders, and other control persons; and

- that enables the creditor to receive more than it would receive in a chapter 7 case if the transfer had not been made—this could occur, for example, when a creditor is paid $25,000 within 90 days prior to a bankruptcy, but in a liquidation the creditor would likely only receive, say, $5,000.

Defenses to a Preference

The Contemporaneous Exchange. A transfer is insulated if it was intended by the debtor and the creditor to be a contemporaneous exchange for new value and if the transfer was, in fact, a substantially contemporaneous exchange. It is not enough simply to show that a substantially contemporaneous exchange occurred. The exchange also must have been intended to be contemporaneous, and it must have been intended as such by *both* parties; for example, this would cover a COD payment.

Payment in the Ordinary Course of Business. This insulates otherwise avoidable transfers to the extent that they were in payment of a debt incurred by the debtor in the ordinary course of business or financial affairs of the debtor and creditor, were made in the ordinary course of business or financial affairs of the debtor and creditor, and were made according to ordinary business terms.

The Subsequent New-Value Exception. A transfer is insulated to the extent that, after the transfer, the creditor gave new value (i.e., supplies new goods or services) on an unsecured basis to the debtor. Essentially, this defense protects the creditor who makes further extensions of credit in reliance on past payments.

Fraudulent Transfer

Elements of a fraudulent transfer. The bankruptcy bode enables the trustee to avoid fraudulent transfers made within one year of bankruptcy. Transfers are avoidable under the bankruptcy code if made with actual intent to hinder, delay, or defraud creditors. Alternatively, a transfer may be *constructively* fraudulent if made for less than "reasonably equivalent value" and made by an insolvent or inadequately capitalized debtor. As in the case of a preference, a transfer is defined broadly to include "every mode, direct or indirect, absolute or conditional, of disposing of property."

Many states have similar laws and have adopted the Uniform Fraudulent Conveyance Act (UFCA). In those states that have not adopted the UFCA, common-law rules or statues closely resemble the federal and uniform statutes. The bankruptcy code also makes state fraudulent-transfer law available to the bankruptcy trustee whenever the transfer took place outside the one-year reachback period contained in the bankruptcy code and within the longer state law period, sometimes reaching up to seven years.

Defenses to a fraudulent transfer. The most common defense to a preference is a transfer in exchange for "reasonably equivalent value." "Value" means property or satisfaction or securing of a present or antecedent debt of the debtor. In other words, unlike a preference, if a payment is made on account of a pre-existing debt, while it might be a preference, it would not a fraudulent transfer.

— ◇ —

Brian Davidoff is the chair of the Bankruptcy, Reorganization, and Capital Recovery Group at Greenberg Glusker LLP in Los Angeles, and is certified in Business Bankruptcy Law by the American Board of Certification. Mr. Davidoff has specialized in corporate reorganization, restructuring, and bankruptcy law for over 30 years and has worked with businesses in a variety of industries, including manufacturing, entertainment, professional services, healthcare, apparel, construction and real estate, food and beverage, and new media. In addition, he has a substantial practice advising companies on the various aspects of their growth, financing, contractual relationships, and operations. In this capacity, he often acts as outside general counsel to his clients. Contact him at bdavidoff@greenbergglusker.com.

2

Experiences in Restructuring

BY HOWARD B. GROBSTEIN

As a young staff accountant, I frequently witnessed my senior colleagues enter situations in which company owners—who had founded and raised great companies and brands—were suddenly in deep, dark trouble, and didn't know how to escape. Like a blockbuster Hollywood drama, all the elements were in play. Angry lenders were threatening to stop funding credit lines or, worse, foreclose. Barking, Pitbull-like suppliers were demanding payment, or refusing to ship products. Frightened salespeople were cowering behind promises, not knowing if they could deliver. And loyal employees were wandering the factory floor like zombies, wondering, "Will I still have my job tomorrow?"

From the sidelines, I watched and thought, "What kind of magic, what kind of hero or heroine, can stave these dark troubles?"

I eventually learned the answer. Each day, my brave colleagues carried with them a potent magic concoction of . . . drum roll . . . solid accounting practices, natural business acumen, and years of experience; enough to turn around fortunes. I was hooked. I knew this was what I was meant to do, too.

Then came the rush of adrenaline I felt when I got my first "real" restructuring assignment. I likened it to that of a para-trooper ready to leap into battle—with nothing but the docu-mentation I studied from the comfort of my desk. Unaware of the terrain and the individuals and challenges I might face, I resolved to be a quick study—to touch down on ground zero, get my bearings, take command of the situation, and complete my mission.

That was 20 years ago.

Although many days I still feel like that adrenaline pumped paratrooper, I now carry the magic with me. That potent con-coction to "save the day."

— ◇ —

In a restructuring, the company often has crippling issues—mismanagement, financial troubles, and sometimes even mal-feasance—that are often so bad that management is willing to pay a team of experts to come in and fix them. Management may know some of the necessary information, such as that sales are down, profit margins are eroding, or the company can't meet its debt obligations. But what management too often does not know are all the underlying details and issues causing these travails. Why are sales down? Is it a product lifecycle issue? Is it because the company lost its competitive edge? Is quality suffer-ing? Is there something wrong with the sales force?

What if expenses are too high? Often management doesn't even realize that the company has experienced expense creep. Do they know if reductions in costs have not been in line with slowing sales?

There can even be sinister issues at play, such as diversion of sales, theft of corporate opportunity, or theft of trade secrets. Worse, is someone in the company stealing?

From an accounting perspective, the big question that always surrounds financial reporting is, "Is it adequate?" Is management obtaining the proper information on which to base operational and strategic decisions? Is the general ledger maintained promptly? Even large companies staff accounting departments inadequately or improperly, which can result in all types of problems, including improper long-term strategic decisions based on faulty information and data.

The restructuring process can mean different things to different companies. In some circumstances, restructuring means trying to save a company from imminent death or bankruptcy. In other situations, it can mean negotiating new terms with lenders to provide the company some breathing space to realign its strategy and survive. Sometimes, the best place for restructuring is in a planned chapter 11 bankruptcy, which has the advantage of being able to force both secured and unsecured creditors to modify the debts owed to them and allow the company to reorganize. For others, restructuring is an orderly winding down—to liquidate the business and make creditors as complete as possible.

Where to Begin

There is no natural entry point. The restructuring team must jump in with both feet to start the process. Because each case is unique, it is essential that the team learns as much as possible, as quickly as possible, to identify the issues and set a course for the desired outcome, whatever that may be. My process includes six key steps, each of which involves a custom-prepared program necessary to meet the restructuring objectives:

1. Perform a background investigation.
2. Visit the company.
3. Interview key people.
4. Get the numbers.
5. Develop an action plan.
6. Work the end game.

First. I conduct a thorough background investigation of the company and its management. I obtain whatever data is available on the company, including information in the public domain, such as articles, financial data, and social media content. From this information, I create a detailed file and flowcharts regarding the organization, and develop a list of preliminary questions and concerns based on my observations.

Second. I walk the floor. I visit the company, meet with management, and "get my hands dirty." I make sure to take a detailed look at the operations, including the back office, c-suite, accounting and finance departments, human resources, sales and marketing, production floor, shipping and receiving facilities, the warehouse, and if applicable, retail space. I observe how the process flows, evaluate employee attitudes, and document my initial impressions. I ask a multitude of questions when I am in doubt or note a particular area of concern. I identify strengths and weaknesses of the organization and its management, and thoroughly document what I am learning and what I need to learn.

Third. I conduct in-depth interviews with relevant individuals, inside and outside the company. I start at the top and work my way down. (Or, vice versa, depending on management tone. If management is adverse toward my presence at their company, I prefer to start at the bottom.) I make sure that I hit all key people in the organization. I take my time to conduct exhaustive due diligence, to get a complete picture. My work often includes meeting with individuals outside the organization, which can be critical to a successful restructuring.

For example, I may set up meetings with the company's outside CPA, the loan officer at the bank, consultants who have been retained to assist with various company matters, and, if relevant, key customers.

The puzzle pieces then start to come together as different pieces of information are cross-referenced.

Fourth. I put my accountant hat on, roll up my sleeves, and get into the numbers. I review and try to understand the company's balance sheet, income statement, and statement of cash flows to create an overview, before digging deep into various other departmental and more specific accounting reports. In this stage, I try to identify anything that stands out on the balance sheet. I usually request two or three years of monthly financial information to make comparisons and immediately mark apparent conditions.

For example, I may see a spike in accounts receivable. Is it because of increased sales or is there a collection problem with a large customer account? I may see dramatic increases in fixed assets. Is the company spending when they should be saving? Are accounts payable growing? Have officers borrowed money from the company? How far behind is the company on its debt service, and can there be forbearance with the lender to get things in shape?

About the income statement, I take time to do the same thing: make comparisons and look for deviations, inconsistencies, or other changes. This activity will drive me into detailed reports that can get to the heart of the issues I previously identified. I observe essential relationships like sales revenue to payroll. If sales have been dropping, is there a corresponding reduction in the workforce or has it grown or stayed flat? I often need to gain a deep understanding of the company's costs of goods sold, and assess the relationship between sales and underlying values. Although the analysis is time consuming, it will answer many questions.

Fifth. I develop an action plan for moving forward, whatever direction that may take. By completing the due diligence and groundwork in steps one through four, I am usually in a strong position to help management start addressing and correcting the issues faced by the company.

I work very closely with my team and the distressed company's leaders. Frequent and thorough communication among these players is critical. When I act as the chief restructuring officer or interim CFO, I often hold daily or weekly all-hands meetings to make sure everyone is on track and important things are getting completed. Also, staying in constant communication with the company's lenders or investors is crucial. I have learned that infrequent or insufficient contact can elevate a sense of uncertainty and break down trust. Equally important is honest, forthright, and frequent communication with the company's employees. They are often taken for granted and left in the dark. They see what's going on and are often fearful of losing their jobs. Taking time to keep them abreast of the situation in a candid way generates trust, and will minimize the rumor mill spiraling out of control.

Sixth. Finally, there is the end game. The plan may be for an out of court reorganization, or it may be to place the company into chapter 11 to reorganize, or to liquidate in a chapter 7. It could be a sale of the assets. And sometimes, the plan may change mid-stride.

If the initial efforts focused on restructuring the company's debt are later found to be infeasible, a shift in strategy may be required. Shifting strategy is not unusual at some point along the course. The key for both owners and consultants is to be nimble and remain unbiasedly observant so that management views the situation in a practical way, one that will yield the best outcome for the company and its creditors.

Real World Stories

With the preceding procedures in place, how does restructuring happen in the real world? Walking through some actual scenarios is helpful.

Jimmy's. Recently, I was retained to consult on restructuring a food distributor and wholesaler. Because the information regarding this case is not public, we will refer to the company with the fictional name "Jimmy's." In this instance, a potential buyer of Jimmy's hired me and split the cost of my services with Jimmy's. Both the buyer and Jimmy's management advised me during brief discussions with the company that it was suffering from a significant drop in sales. They had negotiated a forbearance agreement with the bank, but patience was running thin. The management did not know what to do. The owners were not inclined to sell, so, short of filing for bankruptcy protection, they had few options.

Before heading out to the facility, I searched for available information. Jimmy's is a privately held company, so I was not able to obtain much financial data before my site visit. Still, a simple Google search revealed a significant amount of other pertinent information. For example, I learned that the owners of Jimmy's had other business interests. I learned that one of the owners had substantial real estate holdings independent of the business. This was a clue that he may have given personal guarantees *and* be on the hook for the business debt. I also found several negative comments regarding shipping and supply problems.

Meanwhile, my team reviewed other companies in the same industry, which enabled us to determine where Jimmy's stood among its competition. We also obtained financial data on some of the competitors, which helped us understand the relevant margins, ratios, and other data that we could apply to Jimmy's once we were able to review its actual financial data. We prepared templates into which we could drop Jimmy's data to avoid wasting time when we had access.

In Jimmy's case, much of the research and planning paid off. Upon showing up on site and commencing the interview process, we learned that my hunch regarding personal guarantees was correct. One partner was in a much worse state than the other—he was vulnerable because he had personally guaranteed the debt and also held personal real estate assets that the bank could look to in the event of a default. The other partner had no meaningful real estate holdings and was essentially judgment proof. The difference caused a rift between the owners. They could not readily agree on an approach for change.

After we received Jimmy's financial information, we dropped it into our prepared templates. Almost immediately, we identified significant problems with both the balance sheet and income statement. This development needed our immediate attention. Thankfully, our preliminary research and planning allowed us to jump in and start making changes.

Conducting interviews with relevant parties, both inside and outside the company, is essential. Obtaining an organization chart, if one exists, can form the start of a roadmap for interviews. For smaller or midsize companies, the starting point may be the owners. In larger organizations, it usually makes the most sense to start with the chief financial officers and the chief operating officers and work your way through the ranks. Most of the time, interviewing executives will provide valuable information about operations. More significantly, line employees may have differing views and perspectives on financial and operational issues than their superiors. Such differences can shed a bright light on troubles the company is having. We found this was the case in another company, Organization X.

Organization X. Organization X, a fictional name for a real non-profit organization, was experiencing severe cash-flow problems that did not correspond to increased donor giving. Also, X was going through an extensive, multi-year, multimillion-dollar construction project, in which thousands of project related transactions were being recorded each month, creating accounting intricacies that made the financial standing of the company more difficult to understand. X engaged my team and me to identify the problems.

We started with an interview of the CFO, who seemed well put together and refined. He wore a sharp suit and tie every day and spoke English with refinement, which gave him both an air of confidence and respectability. During the interview, however, his inability to provide detailed information and concise answers to our questions concerned our team. It slowly became clear that he was primarily a figurehead who received financial reports from the controller and transmitted that information to the executive director and the board of directors.

After meeting with the CFO, we interviewed the controller. Unlike the confident CFO, the controller was quite scattered. He had reports with handwritten comments strewn all over his desk and sticky notes as reminders for journal entries. His hair was disheveled and his tie loosened at the neck. He was the epitome of the stereotypical overloaded, overworked, and underwater accountant.

While he insisted he had control over the finances, after questioning the controller admitted that he was behind on updating the general ledger by about three months, had not reviewed the bank reconciliations in about five months, and was overwhelmed with the grueling accounting related to the construction project. He just could not answer why the organization was bleeding when donor contributions had been the highest they had ever been. He, like the CFO, asked that we work to evaluate the income statement to gain an understanding of what was going on with the organization's finances.

After meeting with the controller, we moved on to the accounts payable clerk to understand her perspective on the financial situation within the organization. During the interview, the clerk provided information that had not been set out by either the CFO or the controller. When we inquired about her daily activities, we learned about severe problems related to internal accounting controls at the organization. She described her daily responsibilities, which included no less than being the sole person responsible for opening all of the organization's mail, including the paper bank statements; recording all transactions in the general ledger, including receipts and disbursements; preparing the daily bank deposit and physically walking to the bank to make the deposit; preparing the bank reconciliations on a monthly basis; preparing the donor giving report on a monthly basis; and working with outside auditors, providing necessary reports, annually. The accounting concept of "separation of duties" apparently was not being applied.

We came out of the meeting with the clerk with our heads spinning. At a minimum, this interview yielded invaluable information regarding significant internal control weaknesses within the organization. It also helped us direct our focus as we worked to understand how the bleeding was occurring.

After interviewing the accounts payable clerk, we met with the outside auditors who gave us information that raised more concerns. The auditors indicated that they had previously identified the internal control weaknesses and provided their findings to the CFO and audit committee. They had also identified highly unusual and suspect reports during the audit, that led them to believe there might be embezzlement.

In this scenario, restructuring the actual finances of the company was not necessarily needed; instead, the entire financial reporting process needed a redo. The interviews revealed that basic accounting internal controls were weak or nonexistent, and that oversight at the controller and CFO level was utterly insufficient. Management had no idea that the organization was failing not because of excess expenses but because of a significant employee embezzlement scheme! Our team then restructured the accounting and reporting process and recommended the termination of the employees perpetrating the embezzlement.

When the interview process is complete (and you are not hit by an unusual embezzlement scheme), attention turns to operations and finances. Whether the company is in the business of producing and distributing products or is a service operation, it is important to take a tour of the facility and obtain perspective. From the condition of the facility, the disposition of the employees, and the pace of the operation, warning signs are usually apparent. Often, issues that are troubling companies are clear as day to an outsider who takes the time to walk the production floor with a fresh set of eyes and an open mind, as in the case of Janey's.

Janey's. An apparel manufacturing and distributing company was failing miserably on many fronts—we'll call it Janey's for this illustration. Janey's domestic and international sales were down, yet expenses had increased. The company had defaulted on its loan and line of credit with its lender, and the bank no longer trusted the CFO. They insisted on working with a new and neutral party. Janey's owners called me in to act as their chief restructuring officer and neutral party.

My first action on behalf of Janey's was to introduce myself to the bank and start working on a forbearance agreement, so we could get some breathing room to allow me to take control of the operation.

After conducting initial interviews and learning that sales had declined sharply over the last five years, I set out to tour the facility and get to know and understand each division. I observed operational issues that we could immediately remedy and that would result in savings allowing us to drop additional funds to the bottom line and staunch the financial bleeding.

The company had a 75,000-square-foot warehouse that also housed the business offices, as well as a secondary 20,000-square-foot warehouse about a mile away. Janey's owned the main warehouse and leased the secondary one. During the facility tour, I noticed that while the footprint of the product consumed most of the facilities' available space, the top of the racks was empty and there was available space in both locations. With two years remaining on the lease of the secondary location, and the concept of filing a chapter 11 bankruptcy for reorganization a real possibility, I prepared a budget to move all inventory from the secondary location and condense it into the primary location, immediately stopping payment of the rent on the second facility. The owners, CFO, and COO were all convinced that there would not be enough space in the warehouse for all the company's inventory, but there was. The move cost approximately $20,000, factoring in truck rental and labor, but the savings were enormous and immediately added nearly $30,000 per month in available cash. (Management could have taken this action before entering into the lease on the second building.)

Even if the company was not going to file for chapter 11 bankruptcy—which would allow us to reject the lease and create an unsecured claim—we could still take the same action and attempt to negotiate a settlement of the outstanding lease obligation with the landlord. The threat of bankruptcy in many cases can help resolve these types of issues.

While the process of moving and consolidating the inventory in Janey's situation was relatively simple, most operational issues are not that easy to address. To illustrate, let's look at the case of the (fictional) Water Central company.

Water Central. The water bottling plant—Water Central—was an operating chapter 11 business when they brought me in as a chief restructuring officer. After meeting with top Water Central management, I toured the plant with a focus on the efficiency of the bottling process. With a fresh set of eyes, I looked at everything from water importation, ionization, bottle importation, bottling, testing, labeling, and packaging. I observed a very knowledgeable, hardworking team of employees running the line. I also asked to review the employee files to make sure that everything was in order.

On day two, I had a candid conversation with the chief operating officer and learned that most of the employees had been there for several years, and most were undocumented. Given that this engagement was taking place in a chapter 11 proceeding and that I was now responsible for the operation, I made the very difficult, but compulsory, decision to terminate all the undocumented employees, immediately. The operation was shut down for about a week while I hired and trained new employees.

The forced shutdown was an unexpected challenge at a time when the company was already struggling financially. But during the downtime for hiring and training, I worked with Water Central's COO to go through the entire operation, including sales relationships, defective machinery, shipping and receiving, and inventory aging. We prepared a production capital expenditure budget to determine whether or not it was cost-effective to repair or replace specific pieces of equipment on the line, and then acted on that budget. Once the line was operational, and the new employees were working, we were able to make production significantly more efficient.

Meanwhile, we set up meetings with our largest customers to determine if there were ways to increase sales through their various outlets. One customer, a massive national chain of retailers, had been pressing for higher production and lower cost based on volume but had previously been advised that the line could not handle higher production levels. Now, however, with the capital improvements and new units in place, we were able to increase sales through this very significant distribution channel. We went to other existing customers and in many circumstances were able to reduce selling prices and increase sales volume, resulting in higher revenues for Water Central. We also explored new sales opportunities. We were turning a profit in a matter of about one month after the forced shutdown. The sight of customer tractor trailers pulling in to take the product on a frequent basis was gratifying for me.

Detailed Analysis of Financial Aspects

Any restructuring effort will involve a comprehensive analysis of the financial aspects of the company. The study usually begins with a review of the trial balance, showing summary balances of assets, liabilities, long-term debt, equity, revenue, costs of goods sold, and operating expenses. It provides a general, but helpful, start to an investigation into the financial affairs of a struggling company. From there, other areas of focus, such as oppressive leases, long-term debt renegotiation, and operational issues, can all be explored in greater detail.

After skimming the trial balance and identifying stand-out issues, the process often turns to a more in-depth study of the financials, such as a three-year reverse look on a monthly basis to identify trends, changes, or more unusual activity. From there, problem areas can be examined to more accurately determine issues to correct. This process is the easiest way to spotlight changes that management may be oblivious to, or could not or would not address.

The next step is to prepare a thirteen-week rolling budget, along with budget-to-actual variance analysis. Projections are typically custom built based on the needs and particulars of the company, the secured creditor, and other parties involved in the matter. A secured creditor collateral analysis is commonly part of this projection and will show the creditor's security position, the company's use of cash collateral (the money generated from operations related to the secured creditor's collateral), and the company's ability to continue operations. Also, salary and perquisites for insiders, including officers, directors, and management, are often addressed in these projections. However, a detailed financial analysis is only useful if budget-to-actual comparisons are prepared on a frequent basis and utilized as a tool for taking corrective action.

Restructuring is unpleasant, but it's why restructuring professionals are there. They are brought in to take action that the previous management could not or would not execute for one reason or another, whether that involves simple cost-cutting actions or more aggressive stands, like removing a management role. The success of the restructuring experts require that they make these tough decisions.

Debt and Equity

Debt obligations are often the culprit that forces troubled companies out of business or into bankruptcy proceedings. Restructuring debt and equity is a common restructuring tactic.

In most cases, everyone's best interest is to avoid a complete default of a bank loan and an ensuing bankruptcy. In the best situation, the secured creditor is agreeable to entering into a forbearance to allow some breathing room while negotiations occur to work out terms that are acceptable to the lender and the borrower, avoiding the need to file for bankruptcy protection. But in other cases, the relationship between the parties may be so distressed that such an informal workout is impossible. A severely damaged relationship with a secured creditor that makes the lender unwilling to work with the distressed company leaves management with little choice but to file for bankruptcy protection. A chapter 11 filing will force the company, the secured creditor, and the vendors to try to work out terms under court supervision, which sometimes may be the better alternative for the debtor.

Chapter 11 bankruptcy provides the debtor restructuring alternatives that are not available outside of bankruptcy. (See also chapter 1.) For example, as part of a plan of reorganization, the debtor can attempt to force a "cram down" on a lender by requiring a reduction of interest rates or modification of loan terms. This process may allow for more favorable conditions with unsecured creditors, such as vendors and suppliers, once they realize that the concept of getting something (e.g., a portion of their pre-petition claims as well as ongoing business with a reorganized debtor) is better than nothing at all if the company fails.

Still, attempting negotiations outside of bankruptcy is usually the first choice. A healthy relationship with the secured creditor may result in new terms, such as a change in rates and extended time for payback. This type of loan modification can give the company some flexibility to continue to work with its suppliers and vendors and to operate in the ordinary course, or even on extended terms with them. Without the tri-party cooperation of the lender, the vendors, and the potential debtor, it is extremely challenging to meet cash-flow demands when a company is suffering financially.

Finding New Sources of Money

Finding new sources of money to fund the operations in the forms of debt, convertible debt, or equity is also a common option in bankruptcy. (See chapter 4 for a detailed discussion.) Fresh perspectives on financing can be just what a struggling company needs. New money can take the existing lender out of the process, sometimes at a discount, and allow new parties to work with current management (or replace management) to restructure the business operations and move the company in a more positive direction.

As in the previously discussed case of the water bottling plant, to execute the restructuring plan—replace staff, replace equipment, and increase sales—required funding which the company did not have. To keep the place running while we transitioned to new employees and to pay for the advanced line equipment, we approached a group of individuals who had previously provided the company with short-term financing for specific purposes. Fortunately, we were able to negotiate a financing arrangement whereby these individuals would provide new money and receive a super-priority loan in the bankruptcy case for the money they advanced. A super-priority loan allowed them to be the first ones paid before all other creditors upon confirmation of a plan of reorganization.

The deal worked. We sought and received approval for the transaction from the U.S. Bankruptcy Court. Part of the agreement involved removing existing management and allowing me to remain in control until the newly secured creditors could develop a plan for operating the facility after my exit. In the end, the plan called for the removal of the existing secured creditor, the subordination of the investor's initial debt, entitlement to a super-priority claim for the investors' new money, and partial payment to unsecured creditors upon plan confirmation.

The financially distressed company quickly learns that it is not an easy task to change course on its own. To thrive in a new iteration, whether through a non-bankruptcy workout or a post-confirmation reorganization, requires a certain magic—solid accounting practices, business acumen, a fresh set of eyes, and experience. That is what the restructuring professionals brings to distressed situations. They have the necessary skills to face severe and uncertain issues and manage interpersonal dynamics. They know that no two businesses are alike and to take nothing for granted. Every distressed business has options. Chance should not be one of them.

— ◇ —

Howard Grobstein is the managing partner and co-founder of Grobstein Teeple LLP, an accounting and consulting firm with offices in Los Angeles and Washington, D.C. He is a Certified

Public Accountant, certified in financial forensics by the AICPA, and a Certified Fraud Examiner. Mr. Grobstein has specialized in insolvency, reorganization, and restructuring for over 25 years. During this time, he has represented debtors, creditor committees, secured and unsecured creditors, chapter 7 and chapter 11 trustees. As a member of the panel of chapter 7 trustees in the Central District of California, he regularly acts as a chapter 7 and chapter 11 bankruptcy trustee. He assists businesses that are experiencing financial difficulties by acting as a chief restructuring officer (CRO), chief financial officer (CFO), or consulting with businesses to provide guidance on operational efficiency. Contact him at hgrobstein@gtfas.com.

3

Directors and Officers

BY C. JOHN M. MELISSINOS

Two entrepreneurs grew their business rapidly based on the service they could deliver and their ability to reach new customers. To further their growth, they brought in a partner, and, as they worked together, they continued to expand. In their wildest dreams, they never expected the core business to evolve into so many different service lines. As their closely held business grew and became more complex, their use of lawyers and consultants did not keep pace. Even though they had almost a hundred employees, their accounting, benefits, and payroll systems lagged behind the size of their business. Without a larger management team to help with the ever-growing company, they had to stay laser-focused on day-to-day operations. Meanwhile, their corporate responsibilities lapsed—they were unaware just how much it would matter down the road.

After celebrating 15 years in business, they were blindsided when the venture did not turn out the way they had planned. They were forced to lay off employees and, at the same time, idle a significant amount of expensive, brand new, leased equipment. When they considered selling off some parts of their business to meet their obligations to vendors and lenders, they quickly learned that their lack of attention to critical corporate responsibilities complicated matters, including several contentious lawsuits that they were not prepared to face. It was unclear who had the right to act for the combined venture when the partners disagreed on the next step to take.

Planning before, during, and after a distress situation arises can be the difference between saving your company and being forced to sell or liquidate it—and between personal financial ruin and maintaining control of your destiny.

— ◇ —

Why Legal Relationships and Responsibilities Matter

The legal structure of a business entity is often unnoticeable, particularly in a closely held business. The owner holds executive power, is almost always ultimately responsible for the finances of the company, and has final say over hiring and firing employees. The right to control the company's bank account, and the power to decide which opportunities to pursue and at what price, are usually all held by the entrepreneur who created the company. But as companies grow, and as they take on investment partners or lenders, the duties and responsibilities of the people in charge begin to shift from not just loyalty to themselves and their interests, but a commitment to their financial partners as well.

When companies face business challenges or financial stress, the legal duties of the managers can shift suddenly from maximizing the value of the business to taking the interests of creditors into account. This chapter is about the structures that should be in place before trouble starts, including the legal requirements and boundaries of good corporate governance for a growing business and the required operational standards for officers and directors. This chapter also discusses steps to take in times of distress or when financial clouds appear on the horizon.

Directors, Officers, and Managers of the Company

Unless delegated, a corporation operates under the direction of its board of directors. Frequently, the board delegates much of its authority to the company's officers.

The Role of a Board of Directors. In general, the board's role is to oversee the operation of the company, set policies, supervise the way the president or chief executive officer is going about his or her job, and keep an eye on the long-term health of the company, as well as any longer-term opportunities or challenges. Boards often meet quarterly, and in smaller companies, can act by "written consent" without meeting. Having an even number of directors is disfavored because it can lead to deadlock when a decision is needed, and thus three- and five-member boards are typical, particularly among smaller companies.

Directors are elected by the company's shareholders if it is a corporation. The corporation's bylaws contain the rules controlling how and when they are elected. Having an independent and functioning board can be very important in determining that the company is genuinely separate from another business and from its shareholders for "alter ego" purposes. Indeed, even subsidiaries of relatively large corporations must have their independent boards. A properly functioning board of directors, which in some cases can be just one person, is a legal requirement and should not be evaded, as it protects the shareholders from claims by creditors and customers of the company.

The power of the board of directors is usually not absolute and is more often than not circumscribed by the articles of incorporation and bylaws. Certain matters will typically require shareholder approval, such as the sale of all or substantially all of the assets of the company, a merger with another company, or the dissolution or winding up of the company. Especially in closely held companies, a specific transaction with insiders may also require shareholder consent. It is a director's responsibility, with the input of legal counsel, to understand the limits of his or her authority, as well as when and how they are held accountable to the owners of the business.

The Role of Officers. In contrast to directors, company officers run the business on a day-to-day basis. The precise duties and titles of mandated officers vary from state to state. California law requires that a company have a president/chair of the board, a chief financial officer, and a secretary. In California, and as is typical of other states, unless the articles of incorporation or the bylaws prevent it, a single person can hold more than one of these positions. Many companies will also add vice presidents, controllers, or treasurers to the members of the team running the business. The board of directors appoints officers at its pleasure, although sometimes this authority is delegated to the president.

Typically, an officer can bind the company, and therefore care must be taken in appointing only people who have the maturity and experience to protect the institution. Similarly, once someone accepts appointment as an officer, he has duties and obligations to the company, which if unfulfilled become potential liabilities.

How the Manager of an LLC is the Same (or Different)

Today, many companies are structured as limited liability companies to avoid double taxation and to take advantage of the flexibility that the LLC form affords a business. Limited liability companies can be either "member managed," that is each member is entitled to manage the business of the limited liability company, or "manager managed," in which case the members elect managers to manage the business of the company. However, in larger businesses, the operating agreement governing the LLC can also create executive functions such as the officers of a corporation, and it is not uncommon for executives to hold themselves out as (and, in fact, to be) president, vice president, or chief financial officer of a limited liability company. In that circumstance, the managers will serve in a role similar to that of a board of directors of a corporation.

In more complex entities (and frequently in joint ventures), two or more individuals might serve as managers and make decisions collectively. It is also a common practice for the manager to be another LLC or corporation. Even if you are not personally the manager of the entity in question, you might bear ultimate responsibility for any decisions regarding the business under your authority over any other entities that control the company.

Also, some decisions may require member approval. Typical powers reserved to a vote of the members include a sale of all the assets of the business, incurring debt (sometimes above a certain threshold), or dissolving and shutting down the entity. This list can vary from business to business. As the manager, you must familiarize yourself and be cognizant of the limits of your power, especially if you have third-party members or investors who are not involved in day-to-day management. The failure to make required disclosures to the members, or the failure to secure their approval for decisions which require their consent, can lead to a claim against you—the manager—for breach of fiduciary duty. Merely because a manager is not called director, president, or chief financial officer, does not mean that he or she is relieved from the fiduciary duties to oversee the affairs of the company. As we will see, circumscribed duties may occur in some cases, especially under Delaware law. For the most part, however, a manager of an LLC will have fiduciary responsibilities to the company's members and, in the appropriate circumstances, perhaps even to the company's creditors.

Case Study: The operating agreement governing a 50-50 joint venture formed as an LLC, which was managed by one of the venture partners, authorized the partner/manager to incur debt in the ordinary course of business. However, in a separate provision, the operating agreement also required a vote of the members before the manager was authorized to enter into any financings secured by liens against the property owned by the venture. In need of cash to finance the defense of a lawsuit, but knowing that the other member did not approve of obtaining a loan for that purpose, the manager had to decide whether or not to borrow money secured by the property.

On the one hand, the loan was required for the operation of the business and was within the manager's authority under the first provision of the operating agreement. On the other hand, the loan was to be secured by the property owned by the business, an action for which the second provision of the operating agreement required member approval. Taking advantage of the ambiguity of the operating agreement—which could not anticipate every potential dispute between the members or every possible business scenario—the manager decided to proceed with obtaining the loan and encumbering the property. The immediate need for cash to defend the lawsuit was solved, but the decision opened up the manager to a claim by the other member that the manager had overstepped his authority.

The division of authority between the manager and the members outlined in the operating agreement should always be carefully reviewed upon creation, but also when significant decisions are required or when the company must respond to a legal claim. Otherwise, you may be in for a surprise when you do not have the power to do what you wanted to do, or you need to ask one of your business partners for approval of an action that he or she may be unwilling to give without a critical concession. Conversely, you might be able to use the operating agreement as a "blocking position" to force an action that a manager whom you do not control might not otherwise want to undertake—such as taking on a new loan or selling an asset to raise cash. In either case, the precise language of your agreement may sharply limit your operational flexibility.

The Fiduciary Standard

As formulated by the law of one state, "A director shall perform the duties of a director, including duties as a member of any committee of the board upon which the director may serve, in good faith, in a manner such director believes to be in the best interests of the corporation and its shareholders and with such care, including reasonable inquiry, as an ordinarily prudent person in a like position would use under similar circumstances." This rule, with some variations, generally is applicable in all states.

Directors owe the "duty of care," the "duty of loyalty," and the "duty of good faith" to the corporation. As one court recently put it: The duty of care "is the duty to exercise reasonable prudence in making business judgments for the corporation, including gathering adequate information and undertaking due consideration of the relevant issues." The duty of loyalty means to put the interests of the corporation ahead of those of the director or any other entity. A director who acts for his or her self-interest instead of the interests of the corporation and, thus, its stakeholders breaches this interest. The duty of good faith "is considered part of the duty of loyalty, because directors or officers cannot act loyally toward the corporation unless they act in the good faith belief that their actions are in the corporation's best interest."

The Business Judgment Rule

In interpreting these duties (whether termed two or three), courts will give corporate directors "wide latitude in their handling of corporate affairs because the hindsight of the judicial process is an imperfect device for evaluating business decisions," as a court put it. The policy behind this rule is to allow directors the freedom to act, if they do so without fraud, breach of trust, or self-dealing because it is unlikely that a court's subsequent judgment will be better than that of the directors.

This judicial deference to the decisions of directors is known as the "business judgment rule." In its purest form, the business judgment rule provides that the judgments and actions of directors will not be second-guessed in hindsight, so long as they violate neither the duty of care nor the duty of loyalty. But the protections of the business judgment rule can be lost when decisions are without basis, there are insider dealings, or there is inattention to the duties of a director. One Delaware court formulated the business judgment rule in this way:

A decision by a board of directors (i) in which the directors possess no direct or indirect personal interest, (ii) which is made (a) with reasonable awareness of all reasonably available material information, and (b) after prudent consideration of the alternatives, (iii) which is in good faith, and (iv) which is in furtherance of a rational corporation purpose, will not be interfered with by the courts, either prospectively by injunction, or retrospectively by imposition of liability for damages upon directors, even if the decision appears to have been unwise or have caused loss to the corporation or its stockholders.

What these standards mean, boiled down to their essence, is that if a director acts reasonably based on the (good) information available to him or her (or which the director could have easily obtained), that action should be immune from second-guessing regardless of the result. However, the business judgment rule also presupposes that the director does not have an impermissible conflict of interest that would taint the decision making and cause the safe harbor provided by the rule to be inapplicable.

Case Study: A company operated in the labor and talent-intensive special effects (movie) business. During the Great Recession, the company had the opportunity to obtain a loan on highly favorable terms to purchase its office building. However, as is very common, potential lenders insisted that a separate, "special purpose entity" hold the building. Therefore, the three owners of the company, who were also members of the board of directors, formed a new entity that they owned directly, and then caused the company to loan the new entity the money it needed for the down payment on the property. At the time it purchased the building, the company also entered into a long-term lease with the new entity for the use of the building. The monthly rental payment of rent under the lease enabled the special purpose entity to pay its mortgage. The arrangement was a great deal for the company, allowing it to secure a significant amount of space at favorable rates, in a desirable location, and on a long-term basis.

Several years later, however, the company hit hard times and ultimately filed for chapter 11 bankruptcy. Although the three shareholders had never received one dime from the building purchase transaction, others attacked them for breach of fiduciary duty to the company and its creditors.

Even though they were the only shareholders and thus controlled the business and acted with the best of intentions, the business judgment rule did not prevent a lawsuit from going forward against them on the basis that they had swindled their own company because they had not convened a formal board of directors meeting to approve the transaction nor had they received any opinion on the merits of the transaction.

The lesson here is that even in a situation in which you have the right and power to make the decision, you must still take formal action as a board of directors and back it up with appropriate information and procedure—especially if you could reap some potential benefit from the proposed transaction. You must always keep in mind that everything you do might be reevaluated in hindsight, often under much different market conditions and economic assumptions.

How You Can Protect Yourself

While each set of facts is unique, there are certain steps that you should take to protect yourself in your capacity as a board member, whether you are a principal of the company or an outside director. Each of these steps is crucial to provide a legal defense to you if the decisions you make do not work out and are later challenged.

First, you should insist that the articles of incorporation of the company provide for the indemnification of the officers and directors to the maximum extent permitted by law. Under the laws of most states, this means that the company will indemnify a director for his or her negligent conduct, so long as he or she is otherwise acting in good faith and with fidelity to the company. Although such provisions are standard, they must be included in the company's governing documents before you can call on the company to defend you from a claim. And, while it is true that if the company becomes insolvent and has to file bankruptcy such indemnity rights may be worthless regarding any potential payout, they still might provide valuable rights, claims, and defenses.

Second, you should always rely, to the extent possible, on outside advisors, including lawyers, accountants, and restructuring consultants. You should make sure that if you need advice concerning a particular matter, you obtain it, consider it, and act on it. Even if the result is not ideal, you will have engaged in a thorough analysis and process in arriving at the course of action that the board ultimately adopts. If someone challenges a decision, you can point to the process as indicative of the fairness and reasonableness of the decision, even if it turned out to have been mistaken or improvident. Having a reliable accounting firm is particularly critical because, without knowledge of the true financial situation of the company, you will be unable to make good decisions on its behalf.

Third, make sure that the board is well informed and that it meets regularly. Also, you must memorialize those meetings in written minutes and written resolutions of the board. As part of this discipline, the board should put in place a system to review and oversee the affairs of the company in a way that makes sense under the circumstances, and that will provide you and the rest of the board with the information you need to make informed decisions.

It is also critical to receive and review reports from the various officers of the company. Even in a situation in which a long-standing principal or controlling shareholder is the president and chief executive officer, to rely on the board's actions, the board will have to show that it acted on adequate information. Barebones progress reports from a president or CEO who might also be a guarantor will likely not fulfill a board's duties to obtain the best possible information, especially if the proposed action could be unduly hard on a minority shareholder.

Fourth, as the company's affairs become more complex, it may be prudent to establish standing board committees to provide more detailed analyses of issues that could be sensitive. The most common special committees are financial, audit, and compensation committees. In the case of a transaction that might benefit a controlling shareholder who is also a director, the creation of a committee to review such a transaction will demonstrate the board's good faith in approving it. If necessary, a special committee can have its own advisor, separate from those of the company. Special committees are frequently employed when a company is considering entering into a sale or other transaction in circumstances in which it might later be found insolvent, or when the proposed sale is to an insider or an affiliate. The very existence of a properly functioning special committee might be enough to prevent the assertion of a claim or to defeat a lawsuit in its early stages.

Finally, obtaining and maintaining Directors and Officers, or D&O, insurance is the financial backstop to protect the directors of a company. Although sometimes costly, if nothing else the policy will be available to pay legal expenses for handling frivolous claims. The future of a company is unpredictable and prone to setbacks from competitors, changes in technology, and shifts in customer sentiment. Against this backdrop, the ability to procure and maintain appropriate D&O coverage is something that the board can always control, and ensure that protection is available to the extent possible.

Most D&O insurance policies are "claims made" policies, and various types of notice must be given to the insurer (or sometimes the broker, or both) *before* the policy expires. In the case of a company that is selling itself or shutting down operations due to financial distress, the D&O insurance policy likely will not be renewed. In these circumstances, it is imperative to make a notice of potential claims before the policy expires—even if you are not sure whether there might be a claim. So-called "tail coverage" can also be purchased to extend the reporting period, but often money is tight for a distressed company and tail coverage costly.

In a troubled business scenario, the board should never assume it can obtain a D&O policy renewal or that it can purchase tail coverage. When in doubt, provide a protective notice to the insurance carrier, or make sure that the company's lawyers do it and that you receive a copy of it.

The Red Flags That Should Cause You to Pay Attention

The legal concept of your fiduciary duty to a company can seem complicated, and often it is. On the other hand, in most cases, a board of directors *is* trying to do the right thing and *is* trying to maximize value and make good decisions for the company. Given that reality, and the fact that, especially for a smaller company, using lawyers and consultants at every turn is not realistic, what situations should give a director pause to make sure that more consideration is devoted to protecting all concerned? A few suggestions, as a rough guide, follow.

Insider transactions. Any contract or sale to the principal, a shareholder, or another director warrants a thorough review and a written resolution identifying the business purpose(s) of the transaction. In specific cases, the transaction may require the approval of the requisite percentage of shareholders or members of the LLC. Even if not technically needed, obtaining shareholder or member approval is advisable as a way to insulate directors or managers from liability for a potentially controversial decision.

Sale, merger, or acquisition. The purchase of a new business, the sale of some or all of the company, or a merger should cause a director to make sure that he or she is fully informed and that the transaction makes sense. If you do not have all the facts, get them. The same reasoning applies to purchases of real estate or the entry into significant real property or equipment leases.

Significant potential liabilities, even without a lawsuit. Do not ignore potential liability in any circumstance. Although there are specific guidelines about the timing in recognizing claims for accounting purposes, as stewards of the company it is the job of the directors to make sure that there is a plan for addressing any potential claims arising from a yet-to-be-filed lawsuit. As a director, you may not know all the details of the situation or the reason for the claim, but your ignorance does not absolve you of responsibility: you have a duty to inform yourself of facts that you should reasonably know. It is a rare case in which ignoring a sizable potential liability is a reasonable course of action.

Dividends or Asset Distributions in a Distressed Situation. Directors may be liable for dividends paid when the corporation is insolvent. For these purposes, dividends can include cash payments, in-kind transfers of assets or real property, or even the relief from debt or other liabilities (for instance, allowing a guaranty or a letter of credit to expire without renewal). The precise contours of liability in this area are complicated, but in addition to liability for these distributions, such transfers might also be fraudulent transfers that can be attacked by judgment creditors or even a bankruptcy trustee.

Creditors or Bondholders Committees. Creditors, often bondholders, of larger entities commonly form so-called ad hoc committees whereby they band together and fund the retention of counsel to negotiate with a distressed company. Such committees are almost always seeking information and leverage in further negotiations regarding repayment of their debts. Directors must seek adequate advice when dealing with such a committee.

Majority Stockholder Positions. In addition to the fiduciary duties of a director, a majority stockholder may also owe similar, if not identical, responsibilities to a minority stockholder or stockholders. If you are taking action that will benefit your majority position to the detriment of a minority position, no matter how justified you feel the decision is, it is your responsibility to follow all board of director formalities and obtain appropriate "fairness" opinions, if possible.

Anything that "smells funny." As an experienced business person, presumably, you were asked to be a director of a company for the experience, knowledge, or expertise that you can bring to the company. Thus, you need to trust your instincts about when to make further inquiries. Remember, you are required to make a reasonable investigation, and you must stay informed. In hindsight, your ignorance of the facts will look culpable to creditors and a court.

Case Study: The creator, principal, and CEO of a food processing company had built a substantial business from which he earned an excellent living. However, changing tastes and challenging economic conditions meant that the company was unable to pay its bank loan and was forced to file a chapter 11 bankruptcy case. Despite the protections of the bankruptcy court, the company's operations were to be sold by the creditors, which now controlled its fate. The creditors planned to sell not only the physical operations of the company but also the know-how and techniques that the principal had developed as the basis of the company's business. The principal objected because he believed that this intellectual property belonged to him and that he should retain the value of it, not the company's creditors. Without the intellectual property, the other assets were worth very little.

In a financially distressed situation, the value of physical assets and inventory can evaporate, sometimes seemingly overnight. Meanwhile, the customer relationships, managerial savvy, and intellectual property of a company, including brand names, trade names, trademarks, copyrights, and patents, may represent some of the most valuable parts of the business.

As he built his company, the principal had used that intellectual property to make the company bigger, better, and more profitable. As long as he remained in control of the company, the fact that these processes belonged to the principal and not the company was a distinction without a difference. But once the company was in bankruptcy, the valuable intellectual property became a critical element of potential recovery for creditors.

Of course, the principal had legal rights and perhaps could have proven his rights as superior to those of the creditors. However, the lack of an agreement defining who owned those rights put the principal at a disadvantage, and the principal was forced to abandon his claims and give up his rights to something that very well could have been his.

The Law Governing Your Company Matters

Legacy businesses carry many issues with them, including the form of the entity (i.e., corporation versus LLC) and the law governing its place of establishment. Adequate thought must be given to company formation choices. Legacy businesses often suffer from past decisions that do not mesh with the current needs of management, employees, and the state and geographic scope of business operations. Tax issues aside, a majority of these legacy issues are not relevant to day-to-day operations until the actions of the directors and officers come under scrutiny. That is when its governing laws and the terms of the articles of incorporation and bylaws might make a very big difference indeed. Below, we briefly discuss some of the most common aspects of California, Nevada, and Delaware law, and how they could impact claims against directors and officers.

California. California state law provides a complete set of rules regarding corporations, LLCs, and partnerships. However, because of the prevalence of Delaware entities in California, some California laws are not as developed, or as protective, as the laws of Delaware. However, entities formed under Delaware law with operations centered in California can be subject to California's law.

Nevada. Many companies incorporate under Nevada law. Nevada has lower tax rates and other fees, it has fewer requirements for forming an entity, and less information about the entity must be made public. However, you will need Nevada counsel to form a Nevada entity, and you will also owe fees every year to Nevada to maintain your corporate status. In multi-subsidiary businesses, you may find that some of them are Nevada entities. Depending on the circumstances facing a company, this might be a significant benefit or a potential burden.

Delaware. Delaware is a favored state in which to incorporate. The reasons for this are that Delaware has developed an extensive body of corporation-friendly laws and the Delaware Chancery courts have developed a significant level of expertise in corporate and business matters. Furthermore, financing sources, vendors, lenders, and others all have a high comfort level with Delaware's rules. If you are starting a new business today, and especially if you intend to operate in more than one state, you should at least consider Delaware as a potential corporate jurisdiction. Of course, for out-of-state businesses, organizing in Delaware means additional cost. But the trade-off can be worthwhile.

For officers and directors, many believe that Delaware law offers them more protection than California law because the contours of the business judgment rule are more developed and more uniformly applied by Delaware courts. So if you are hoping to attract a skilled outside director to help guide your business to the next level, the application of Delaware law might make it easier to recruit the individual you want. By the same token, if you are in a situation in which third parties are questioning your actions, and you know that Delaware law applies, you should carefully analyze the scope of the defenses which may be available to you.

As you think through these issues, you should consider engaging the assistance of a knowledgeable business lawyer.

Together, you are more likely to make the best decision for your circumstances.

The Particular Flexibility and Protections Offered by Delaware LLCs

Not without reason, Delaware law makes that state one of the most popular choices when forming an LLC. Limited liability companies established under Delaware law are common business vehicles. Companies choose to form LLCs in Delaware because they offer flexibility, protections that can be built in for the entity's managers, and the ability to indemnify and disclaim liability for duties and actions that might otherwise give rise to liability.

Under Delaware law, a manager may operate an LLC, but the LLC can also create a board of directors and officers, just like a corporation. The operating agreement of a Delaware LLC can also limit its manager's (or managers') liability and fiduciary duties to the other members and indemnify the managers for any liability that does arise. Also, Delaware law allows an operating agreement to permit the manager to enter into related-party transactions without necessarily breaching the fiduciary duties of the manager. While both California and Nevada law offer similar flexibility, the Delaware business laws are the most familiar, and many believe the most business-friendly of any state.

When you become a manager, officer, or even director of a Delaware LLC, make sure that you read and understand (to the extent any non-lawyer can!) the operating agreement's delineation of your duties and responsibilities, as well as the limitations of them. You might also learn that other parties who you thought had specific duties to you (for instance, in the case of related-party transactions, sales, or financings) do not have those duties or have disclaimed them. Finally, there should be at least some residual authority that remains with the members of the LLC. You should be aware where your authority ends, and that of the members begins, and what, if any, disclosure obligations you have to the members.

Corporation, LLC, or Partnership?

The decision about which type of organization you want—for instance, a corporation (S or C), LLC, or partnership (limited or general) is a decision that you need to make based on the circumstances of your business. Often, the choice about which entity to use is tax- or investor-driven. In most cases, by the time the business is in distress, there is no way to change the form of the entity.

In closely held companies, it is common in the case of corporations for the shareholders to enter into "shareholder agreements" regarding the disposition and voting rights of the equity in the company in a given set of circumstances. It is imperative that you obtain and scrutinize any such agreement that does exist.

LLCs as vehicles for joint-venture arrangements are common, and they can contain very complex buyout provisions. To determine enforcement, however, an analysis by experienced counsel is necessary. Such provisions often have very tight timelines and very particular requirements about when to invoke them, the steps to take, and funds to pay. In a distressed business, some of the assumptions in these provisions may no longer make sense, or may even have the opposite effect: a provision meant to protect one party might actually now help the other. Like shareholder agreements, it is critical to review these "buy-sell" provisions thoroughly. You can assume that any partner with whom you are no longer in agreement is carefully examining them.

As discussed above, in a corporation or an LLC you will find that the managers, partners, and directors will owe fiduciary duties to operate the business for the benefit of the stakeholders. If you are unsure of the scope of the duties of your position, you need to determine what those parameters are as soon as possible. Ignorance of what you were supposed to be doing will not be an excuse once you are the object of a claim.

When Duties to Your Creditors (Including Your Lender) Can Arise

Over the last 20 years, a great deal of time and energy has been spent evaluating exactly when, if ever, directors must consider the interests of the *creditors* of a company, as opposed to its shareholders. The rules have evolved and changed over time, with the courts of Delaware leading the way. In general, it is the case that once a corporation is insolvent, the stakeholders are the creditors, not the shareholders—because the entity's debts are so significant that no shareholder value remains. In this situation, directors must exercise their fiduciary duties consistent with the interests of creditors. Put another way, once the company is insolvent, directors must make decisions that do not unduly risk creditor recoveries.

As discussed in other chapters, one way of discharging this duty is to file a bankruptcy case or enter into an assignment for the benefit of creditors. Sometimes it is clear that only a bank or other secured lender has any hopes of recovery from the assets of the failing business. Neglecting to take that reality into account can lead to liability (even personal liability), and consideration by the board of directors is required any time a significant credit line or bank loan goes into default.

Other more complicated circumstances can also arise, such as when a lawsuit threatens the company or when the loss of a valuable customer means that the viability of the business comes into question. In these cases, boards of directors must seek legal advice and ensure that they are discharging their fiduciary duties appropriately. It may be that the business can be restructured and survive, but directors should always have a contingency plan available if a turnaround is not possible. The passage of time in these situations is likely your enemy. In hindsight, the failure to take action when the business still has options is usually worse than just making a wrong decision. Often, the sale of the company is the only alternative, but it must also be carefully considered by the board to ensure its fairness to the shareholders or creditors.

Although it is likely to be tempting, resigning from the board when faced with such a decision is almost never a good option. Abdicating your responsibility just when the business needs it most will not be considered to be a benefit to the company, and it is likely that previous actions, or failures to act, by board members have already set the stage for a potential lawsuit.

But for directors who have faithfully discharged their duties, things are not so bleak. The business judgment rule—and hopefully D&O insurance—ultimately should insulate them from any adverse claims.

— ◇ —

John Melissinos is a partner at the law firm Greenberg Glusker Fields Claman & Machtinger LLP in Los Angeles. Mr. Melissinos practices in all areas of bankruptcy law, representing debtors, creditors, trustees, committees, and other interested parties in chapter 11 cases, bankruptcy-related litigation, and complex chapter 7 matters. He is experienced in representing distressed companies as they seek to restructure or dispose of business units, including those in the entertainment, retail, food, and residential building industries. Contact him at jmelissinos@greenbergglusker.com.

CHAPTER

4

Leading the Financially Distressed Company

BY MARK LEFKO

The bad news for Tom Szaky and his company, TerraCycle, arrived in March 2007. The eco-friendly, fast-growing start-up company that manufactured liquid fertilizer made from worm droppings and used recycled soda bottles as packaging was sued by the 800-pound gorilla of the fertilizer industry, Scotts Miracle-Gro Company. That year, Scotts logged over $2.7 billion in annual revenues, while TerraCycle had not even been profitable yet. The lawsuit accused the start-up of false advertising and stealing the look and colors of its packaging.

Although TerraCycle had developed a solid reputation for efficacy and sustainability in just under six years, and its products had found their way onto the shelves of major retailers across the United States, it now faced the possibility of trying to fight a lawsuit against a well-heeled corporate behemoth. That prospect was sure to squeeze the company's already limited financial reserves—cash was tight. Payroll would be a question mark, and acquiring additional financing was a long shot. Szaky had some tough decisions to make. The odds did not appear to be in his company's favor. He seriously contemplated that he might have to shut down the business.

Under similar situations, most leaders would follow their first instinct: hide the news from the rest of the company, and possibly the firm's partners and customers. The assumption is that when people hear bad news, they flee. But Szaky, a Canadian by birth who had dropped out of Princeton to co-found TerraCycle, didn't hunker down with his executive team and investors to keep things quiet. Quite the opposite. He decided to open up to his entire staff of 33 employees and tell them about the company's new challenge.

When Szaky shared the news with his people, the shock hit like a freight train. But, rather than handing in their resignations, his employees vowed to join him in the fight to keep their company alive. Not only that, every employee came to him and volunteered to take a pay cut to help keep the company solvent. They committed to weathering the storm, together.

All things considered, Szaky and his team decided it was in the company's best interest to open up the news even further. They created a public-facing website called "suedbyscotts" (no longer active) as a way to let *all* of their stakeholders—retail partners and customers included—know what they were up against. The media, including many bloggers, quickly picked up the story and began spreading it further and further.

Eventually, TerraCycle and Scotts reached a settlement whereby TerraCycle agreed to change the packaging of its products. Surprisingly, the company emerged stronger as a result. Not only had it survived its darkest time, but the team also became even more committed to the company's sustainable mission. If that were not enough, the TerraCycle brand reaped a considerable amount of goodwill and public relations value— greater than it could ever have paid for on its own—by acting in a very forthright and honest manner about its challenges.

TerraCycle not only beat the odds, today it thrives.

— ◇ —

Doing Well by Doing Good

I initially spoke to Tom Szaky about his company while researching my book *Global Sustainability: 21 Leading CEOs Show How to Do Well by Doing Good* (Morgan James Publishing, Jan. 2017). Tom's conscious approach to leading his business from a struggling start-up into a global brand struck me. What I hadn't realized, but later learned, was how close his company had come to shutting down in the wake of the lawsuit brought by its biggest competitor.

As part of my research for this book, devoted to helping financially distressed business owners, I spoke with Tom again, hoping to dig deeper into his motivations and actions as he pulled his company out of its death spiral. Ultimately, it became clear that his *conscious leadership* was the key. In this chapter, we explore his, and others, experiences in conscious leadership, to encourage and guide all businesses, particularly those experiencing distress.

Conscious Leadership

A conscious leader has a purpose that drives him or her and also inspires the team. A conscious leader connects with his or her people in a way that can boost the bottom line without sacrificing integrity or compromising the company mission. A conscious leader always strives to do the right thing. Although conscious leaders are by no means perfect, when they make mistakes they clean them up right away.

I asked Tom about his decision to show his hand to employees and stakeholders when his company faced financial uncertainty. He explained his thinking to me this way:

> I thought that if I tried to keep problems in a small group and not disclose the truth, it could create more problems. People will make up their own worst-case scenario stories anyway. I decided it was more important to be completely and brutally transparent and make everyone feel a part of the challenge we were facing, even if they didn't necessarily want to hear it. I learned that by opening up, people were willing to make personal sacrifices to help in our mission, which was way better than me having to force that kind of reduction on everyone.

Leading consciously may not always be the most natural approach, but it is proven to be effective. Although there are many different schools of thought when it comes to deciphering what makes an active leader, I believe that the best leaders are conscious leaders. I have seen it firsthand in my roles as a corporate employee and leadership consultant and facilitator.

A conscious leader is aware that whatever is said or done will have an impact on everyone and everything around him. Therefore, a conscious leader will consider all stakeholders— employees, customers, suppliers, investors, bankers, families, and communities—with the intention of making decisions that are in the highest and best interest of all. Through the course of TerraCycle's troubles, Tom's choices started his company's financial turnaround much faster than anyone could have hoped. The extreme test of his company's survival resulted in TerraCycle's becoming a company with which other companies and consumers wanted to do business.

Clearly, in situations of financial distress, there are circumstances when communicating with external parties may be ill-advised, or even illegal. But keeping the communication lines open with one's internal stakeholders—especially during tough times—is a critical step in leading a turnaround. As Tom's story illustrates, one can beat bad odds by walking the walk of a conscious leader.

To be sure, one still has to focus on the fundamentals of the financial restructuring, but organizations can, in fact, dig out from difficult financial situations and set the agenda to thrive once things have turned around when conscious leadership is in place.

Are You a Conscious or Unconscious Leader?

I've had the opportunity to interview hundreds of business leaders throughout my career. Great business leaders don't usually start out being great. They get there through hard-earned lessons and a constant dose of self-awareness.

For example, to be a conscious leader, you not only need to know what that *is*, more importantly, you also need to know what it *isn't*. Entrepreneur, life coach, and business consultant John Wood, based in Perth, Australia, gives us an excellent roadmap.

Unconscious Leaders

7. Their authority is externally based on structure, position, rank, affiliations, and the imagined trappings of power. Winning matters above all else.

8. They are frightened. Unspoken fear drives them to seek the illusion of power. They live in the conditioned belief that their survival is always under threat, so they seek security in power and influence as compensation.

9. At best, they pretend to listen. They hear words, but are rarely touched by them. They are unaware of the authentic individual in themselves or others. They are threatened by difference.

10. They vacillate, give in to pressure, have no sense of the difference between substance and style, what is true, and what is false. Expedience, personal power, self-preservation, or blind commitment to the party line drive their leadership style.

11. They promote themselves or invoke some external authority—often with blind arrogance. They are focused on being right and making others wrong. They are self-absorbed and self-centered.

12. They live by second-guessing—their own decisions and those of others. They do not access the original thinking and wisdom that lies within each human being.

13. They try to control life. They will do whatever it takes to get what they feel they need to survive or further their causes.

14. They have little or no faith in the deeper intelligence behind life. Their illusions of control, power over others, and manipulation (in one form or another) are what they believe will work.

15. Their insecurity governs their behavior. Loyalty is absent in their leadership style.

16. They think that life is happening to them—with no awareness that they are creating their own lives.

Conscious Leaders

1. They experience authentic power. Their power is internally based. Their wisdom and common sense guide their decisions. Their innate self-confidence is recognized by others as the purest form of power.

2. They appear fearless. Although they experience fear, as all people do, they are not governed by it and simply use it to channel their energy and efforts.

3. They are extraordinary, active listeners. They are curious about and listen deeply to others. They encourage those who have different realities to express their views, fully and frankly. They are not threatened by those differences.

4. They demonstrate integrity in their wisdom and common sense. They are connected to their inner world, their deeper intelligence. They listen primarily to this inner authority— the source of wisdom within each of us. They effortlessly hold firm in the face of difficulty, even as others around them lose their bearings.

5. They are vanguards—champions for the advancement of their colleagues, their communities, for the greater good. They are courageous yet humble in sponsoring what they see will assist their stakeholders.

6. They are not blind followers. They don't "toe the party line," making independent decisions, maintaining their integrity even when pressured to vote with the in-crowd, while relying for guidance on accumulated wisdom and common sense.

7. They have faith that life presents what is required for fulfillment. They are flexible, resilient, patient, and secure in knowing that what is needed will be at hand.

8. They have faith—in themselves, in their colleagues, in

humanity. And beyond themselves, they have faith in life itself.

9. They personify loyalty. Even when practical realities demand that they make difficult decisions, including personnel decisions, they do so with integrity and conscience.

10. They are awake to life. They understand that all their experience is created from within their own minds, moment to moment, and rejoice in life as an ever-unfolding creative process.

Establishing Guiding Principles

The first and most important element for becoming a conscious leader is to know what you stand for. You should be able to communicate your organization's values to your employees, your customers, your shareholders, and the world at large. Who are you? What drives you, besides the bottom line? What commitments are you willing to make and stand by, regardless of what happens? Are any of these commitments so vital to your company's identity that you are eager to keep them, even at the expense of your ability to maximize profits?

These are not merely abstract questions. The answers will determine how you conduct your business for decades to come, both in lean times and during periods of prosperity. Your values will guide every business decision you make, and their importance to your brand cannot be overstated. Consider that TerraCycle's guiding principles—ridiculous transparency, fierce innovation, and hard work—are all tied to their mission of "Eliminating the Idea of Waste®" by recycling the nonrecyclable.

"What we do as a company is a more important aspect of who we are," Tom told me when we talked. These aren't just empty words. Even as he thought his company might fail, it was essential for him to be true to his guiding principles.

"I used to hold things close to the vest," he said, "but then I decided that making things more transparent helped employees feel engaged and more understanding of where they fit into company profitability." Tom even shares the company's financials with employees and encourages them to "think big" by setting a tone that supports creativity and empowerment to chase new opportunities that no one had thought of.

Enacting and abiding by guiding principles during financial distress can be risky, mainly because it may appear to shareholders and others that you are losing money—at least in the short term—by sticking to your principles. In this regard, small companies can sometimes have an advantage over big corporations. The collective will of countless shareholders can act as an impersonal force of nature, making it difficult or outright impossible for leaders to follow the dictates of their consciences. By contrast, a small operation—or even a very large one, if it is privately-held—is accountable to fewer people, and in some cases, the CEO may have no one's money at stake but his or her own.

The point is that no matter how others may pressure you to act, as a conscious leader it is critical to stand by your guiding principles as a way for your stakeholders, especially your employees and customers, to know what you stand for—in good times and bad. It might have been tempting for Tom Szaky to stop sharing the company's financials with his employees when the company's struggles began, but he didn't. He stayed true to his belief in the power of transparency, not only with his employees but also with all stakeholders. When you lead with that kind of authenticity, you reap more significant dividends over the long run than if you were to compromise your principles for a short-term gain.

Conscious Leadership Principles Matter to Your Employees

While it is admirable for a company to set ambitious goals—such as pulling itself out of a financial hole or fighting off its greatest competitor—it can only *hope* to achieve such goals if its employees are *not* willing to adopt them as their own.

Employees are the lifeblood of any organization. If they are not supported and taken care of, an organization is unlikely to achieve its goals, financially or otherwise. Few business concerns are more important than employees' health, safety, engagement—and *motivation*. Employees who feel respected and trusted will go to surprising lengths to earn and keep their employer's respect, even during tough financial times. But for this to happen, employees must sense that the company takes its principles seriously and that those principles arise from sincere convictions.

Employees who are inspired by a company's mission—and who understand the reasons behind that mission—will further it. The company should communicate its values to prospective employees during the hiring process. Applicants who evince an affinity for the company's goals, not just in business (which of course is a job requirement) but also in matters of principle are optimal.

To the degree that principles are important, it is also paramount to remember that people are only human. Despite best intentions and the most careful hiring practices, bad apples may be hired, or good employees—sometimes even the best employees—may experience lapses in their good judgment.

Consider the views of David MacLennan, the CEO of Cargill, the privately held industrial giant based in Minnesota.

Sometimes your guiding principles are violated, and we're not naïve enough to think that with a large company of 150,000 employees in 70 countries things always go the way that they should. What we attempt to cultivate is a culture of candor and a culture of openness, and we rely on the guiding principles for us to be in business and for us to be trusted. In a values-based company, when you have a violation of your guiding principles, you need to move quickly to respond to it. We had a situation where someone didn't manage their budget in a way that was consistent with our guiding principles, and they were asked to leave the company. And it was done quickly and without hesitation. I think how you respond to violations of your guiding principles ultimately defines your culture.

When guiding principles become ingrained in your culture, your company's values and ethical standards become a selling point to attract and retain talented, ambitious people. Most people are looking for satisfaction and meaning in their lives. People need to feel that they are valuable members of the societies in which they live, and that the contributions they make to those societies *matter*. When we know we have done good work—and when our satisfaction in a job well done is validated with praise, encouragement, and the opportunity to take on more challenging responsibilities—the chemical dopamine floods our brains.

Dopamine is part of the brain's reward system, which serves to reward and reinforce desirable behavior. The pleasure we derive from a dopamine rush is addictive. The upshot is that if we are recognized and rewarded for excellent work, we will redouble our efforts to continue to earn such recognition, especially when those contributions are tied to the organization's mission.

In short, happy employees are more productive employees. Employees who understand themselves to be valued team members are more confident and relaxed, and therefore, more innovative and energetic. Such employees invariably provide better customer service, which results in happier customers, which leads to more business and higher profits. Employees in a state of perpetual anxiety will have the opposite effect.

What happened at TerraCycle when Tom Szaky opened up to his employees with brutal transparency is the perfect case in point. Rather than lose employees, or see productivity wane due to the stress of the situation, the TerraCycle team rallied together with management to take on the most significant threat they had ever faced. That threat, Tom told me, created solidarity among his team when they needed it most. "It became a rallying cry for us," he said.

Conscious Leadership Principles Matter to Your Customers

Some readers may recall Volkswagen's global scandal, when the company admitted to equipping 11 million diesel engine cars with software designed to cheat emission tests. The consequence of this breach of consumer trust was catastrophic.

According to major financial news outlets, such as Bloomberg and *The New York Times*, in the immediate aftermath of the revelation, Volkswagen posted its first quarterly loss in 15 years, after losing 23 percent of its value overnight. Since the 2015 scandal broke, the company has been forced to set aside billions to cover the costs of making the affected vehicles compliant with emissions laws.

As chilling as it is to contemplate the financial repercussions of Volkswagen's mistake, the longer-term damage to the automaker's reputation is perhaps more significant. A survey conducted by research and consulting firm AutoPacific confirmed that by October 2015, only 25 percent of Americans had a favorable view of Volkswagen, down from 75 percent before the scandal.1 By December, the automaker reported that American sales had dropped 24.7 percent in November compared to the same month in 2014. That's a significant signal from customers, letting the company and the world know how they feel about being lied to.

The lesson from the Volkswagen story is clear: treating customers with respect means more than just greeting them with a smile when they walk into your business. It means dealing with them honestly and ethically and working to earn their trust. At a minimum, this means not lying to them.

Consider the difference in how TerraCycle treated their customers in the wake of their lawsuit. They opened up and kept all stakeholders in the loop as the negative event unfolded. As a result, the company gained customers. Through the attention it was receiving from the lawsuit, customers picked up the cause of "David versus Goliath." Many actively chose to purchase TerraCycle products over larger and more established competitors. The positive outcome, in part, is attributed to the company's CEO, Tom Szaky, who embraced the conscious leadership position of trusting his customers with the truth.

---

1 Deborah Grieb, "Volkswagen Reputation Takes Big Hit with Vehicle Owners," AutoPacific, Oct. 2015, http://autopacific.com/news-app/story.248/title.volkswagen-s-reputation-takes-big-hit-with-vehicle-owners-autopacific-predicts-tough-road-ahead/menu.no/sec./home (Last accessed June 2017).

Conscious Leadership Principles for Organizational Growth

CEOs can fall victim to the tremendous pressure to develop short-term strategies for short-term results. We know that this often comes at the expense of all stakeholders' long-term interests. In fact, the pressure for quarterly results is usually in direct conflict with sustainable initiatives and investments that enable long-term growth and profitability. Shortsightedness can jeopardize an entire industry. This is true both regarding resources—imagine how long the timber industry would last if it never planted new trees to replace those it cut down—and financial matters.

The conscious leader plans for the future—not the sole pursuit of short-term results and instant gratification—by striking a balance between short-term earnings and long-term investments. Finding this balance requires courage on the part of CEOs, who must communicate with shareholders, bankers, and other investors the importance of ensuring that their investments are sustainable in the long run.

Most people think they understand what long-term thinking is and why it's important, but tend to practice it selectively. That kind of myopia isn't going to cut it. A business that focuses only on short-term profits will never grow to reach its real potential or achieve maximum profitability. People who don't consider the long-term consequences of their actions or who fail to change direction when headed for a cliff will fall. But a conscious leader recognizes the potential return on investment in planning for the future. And in that, there is no limit to the profit his or her company can realize.

Consider what Blake Mycoskie, the founder of TOMS Shoes—famous for its "buy one-give one" program—has to say about the importance of keeping the long-term in mind:

It's not just the right thing to do morally; you'll actually make more money down the road if you take a more sustainable approach. Your customers will be more like evangelists, your employees will be more engaged and productive, and you'll find that other businesses are more encouraged to partner with you because they like what you're doing. I always say, don't look at this as a cost; look at this as an investment with a very high return on that investment. It might be a longer-term ROI, but it will come.

Conscious Leadership and the Adaptive Business

Anyone who hopes to survive in business must learn to adapt—not if, but when. Conditions in your market or sector will inevitably change. If public demand for your product or service changes, or can be expected to change, you can't just pretend it isn't happening. Consider what happened to Blockbuster Video when they failed to anticipate how the public would respond to Netflix. By the time Blockbuster recognized the danger they were in and made a few clumsy attempts to adapt to the public's desire for an easier way to rent movies, it was too late.

Or imagine what might have happened if the taxicab industry had the foresight in 2009 to design phone apps to summon cabs. They eventually did this, but it wasn't enough to protect their monopoly, and it may yet emerge that it is too late for their industry, completely.

It turns out that TerraCycle is also a prime example of a company that needed to adapt for the long run. Although the company weathered its immediate legal issues, afterward it had a difficult time scaling to the size that could take on a giant competitor like Scotts in the marketplace. But Tom Szaky, again, took a page from his conscious leadership play-book and opened the challenge to his employees: Help us find a way to fulfill the company's long-term mission to "recycle the unrecyclable."

To Tom, dark moments can be an excellent opportunity to be innovative, and it's essential to make room for that. He said, "It's better to innovate your way out of tough times than to fight your way out by clinging to the way you've always done business."

For TerraCycle, that meant radically rethinking their business model. They knew that to scale up their product any further presented a possibly insurmountable challenge. Instead, they adapted by shifting to services. Today, the company teams with a variety of private and public sector organizations across 21 countries to make recycling otherwise unrecyclable items economically feasible.

For example, every year billions of cigarette butts end up in dumpsters and landfills or get tossed as litter on shorelines, parks, and sidewalks. TerraCycle, staying true to its mission, invented a method to recycle cigarette waste at a time when no one thought that was possible. The company now works with every major tobacco company and has developed a free and sustainable process for collecting discarded butts, including a receptacle program that is deployed in dozens of U.S. cities. The cigarette filter waste collected through this program is recycled into a variety of industrial products, such as plastic pallets, and any remaining tobacco becomes compost.

In another example, the company pitched to large office supply retailers the idea of running in-store programs to recycle notebook binders, which removes tough-to-recycle material from landfills. Initially, retailers, such as Staples, said no.

"For Staples," Tom said, "recycling notebook binders was an 'unknown.' The service did not exist, and no one knew if there was a market for it."

Eventually, Staples took the leap and listed the service, which became not only a good thing for the company's social mission but also a very high revenue-generating platform for them. The recycling centers drive foot traffic to Staples locations and are now replicated by other retailers.

Shifting a business model is probably the toughest—and riskiest—thing a company can do. It takes vision and long-term thinking. When I asked Tom what his greatest challenge was in initiating the company's new service model, he said, "getting partner companies to overcome initial doubts." Would anyone even *want* this? Would it work? Would people pay to recycle something that they can toss out for free? The answer is, increasingly, yes.

By using tough times as a catalyst for change, TerraCycle evolved from offering products, to partnering with other organizations to recycle the unrecyclable. By sticking to principles and engaging its workforce in a meaningful way, the company found a way to turbocharge their growth. Tom Szaky exemplifies conscious leadership in action. He was able to adapt and pivot his company just a few years after weathering a significant lawsuit and financial uncertainty.

Even during the toughest of times, the conscious leader can find a way to come out ahead and be stronger than ever.

KEY TAKEAWAYS

- Your guiding principles and brand are inextricably linked. It becomes the public's perception of your stance.

- Open communication, especially with internal stakeholders, helps reinforce your mission and loyalty among team members.

- Your reputation for doing business in a principled, ethical way can help you attract and retain talented, valuable employees. Similarly, trusted companies draw customers.

- Shortsightedness in pursuit of immediate profit paradoxically harms the long-term profitability of a business.

- Transparency and candor open up opportunities for innovation and adaptation. Allowing company stakeholders to take part in steering a company's turnaround is good business.

— ◇ —

Mark Lefko, founder of the Lefko Group (www.LefkoGroup. net) is a leading facilitator for corporate retreats, CEO peer groups, and corporate conflict resolution. He has coached and mentored hundreds of CEOs and business leaders, and has led countless strategic planning retreats, team-building sessions, corporate think tanks, and corporate conflict resolution sessions. Mr. Lefko is known for his high-energy, high level of consciousness, and incisive professional and personal guidance. He intends to lead by example and uphold the highest level of integrity, creativity, and collaboration. In 2012 he founded the Conscious Leadership Connection, and is the author of *Global Sustainability: 21 Leading CEOs Show How to Do Well by Doing Good*. You can reach him at mark@lefkogroup.net or 805-857-4899.

5

Turnaround Accounting

BY SAMUEL R. BIGGS

L ife is mostly a guessing game, in that none of us know with certainty what the next day, year, or even moment may hold. Barring our efforts to exert some control over our circumstances and the environment in which we operate—through the education levels we achieve, the health in which we maintain our bodies, and the manner in which we behave—we cannot entirely control our destinies. We may develop our own unique goals, incentives, and behaviors in order to minimize uncertainties, but external influences will often prevail. Therefore, we learn to operate and handle all that life throws our way on a daily basis, while learning from our mistakes and gaining new knowledge to achieve our goals and objectives.

To a great extent, operating a business is much like life—full of uncertainty and unknowns. Although a business activity may flourish by happenstance for a brief period, a truly successful enterprise can never exist in this manner for any duration. Successful business owners must continuously manage, control, and direct operations to strategic ends through understanding business operations, markets, and objectives. They must obtain information, monitor operations, study the markets, and plan for the future. They must work to gain as much knowledge as possible of every aspect of their businesses and the market to plan for the future, optimally.

— ◇ —

Knowledge is Power

Ipsa scientia potestas est—knowledge is power—is an expression attributed to Sir Francis Bacon that describes the driving necessity for all business managers to be acutely of every element of their businesses and the market factors that affect them. Every business owner should keep this concept at the forefront of his or her mind. For the more knowledge you have, the more likely you are to succeed.

Knowledge is what you get when you combine information—facts provided or learned about something or someone—with analysis and experience. Knowledge is information distilled down to actions.

One of my favorite responses, when I'm asked what I want for any special occasion, is, "Next year's *Wall Street Journal*." If it were ever possible to magically obtain this gift, I would have all the precise information I'd need to know about where the markets are headed. I could then distill this information and know exactly where to invest my funds for the upcoming year.

Of all the various contributors of knowledge to the business manager, and the one most fundamental and readily maintained, is the information provided through the accounting system. The accounting system is the most objective and probably the most integral to the business, but frequently the least attended to, particularly in the troubled company. The accounting system can be one, if not the first, that will indicate problems. But if the system doesn't exist, or management ignores it, there is very little hope that issues can be identified in time to restructure the business. Failure to understand the value of accounting systems is the most common characteristic of the troubled company.

Another common expression that comes to mind is, "A little knowledge is a dangerous thing." The business manager may understand accounting systems and their necessity in effectively managing business operations, but may be fearful of what might be learned and, thus, choose to disregard the signals of a troubled business. A fine example is a person who rushes to buy that "perfect new home" without first getting an inspection, because of "missing the opportunity." Only after closing on the sale does the buyer later learn that he has purchased a disaster.

Unfortunately, many troubled businesses are managed by individuals who lack accounting skills and do not understand the financial controls and statements necessary to manage a profitable business. Sometimes this is the result of the manager's lack of training in this area; sometimes it's due to misplaced priorities on sales and marketing, relegating accounting to a minor administrative function. Sometimes the manager may not want to be controlled by accounting and financial parameters. Whether these or other elements are consequential to accounting deficiencies, a manager or owner of a troubled business must recognize that accounting deficiencies are somewhere at or near the root of the problem, and the financial functions must be addressed in the business turnaround.

Accounting is King

Success in business requires determination, passion, and expertise—and sometimes a little luck. Beyond this, what most successful business owners have in common are reliable systems to help them manage their enterprises. When it comes to managing a business, accounting is the company's central nervous system, and its health is essential.

A company's accounting system will send messages when it is on the right track, and also when it is on the wrong track. At the slightest sign that a company is heading in the wrong direction, the observant business owner acts fast. He or she knows that accounting issues are like wounds. If left untreated, they fester and can get nasty, pretty quickly.

Fortunately, a business will give plenty of warning signals before it experiences acute financial distress. Not watching for those signals, ignoring those signals, or, for various reasons, being unwilling or able to respond will surely land a company in financial trouble.

To frame it a different way: when you are sick, your body is telling you that something, somewhere in your system is wrong. In most cases, confronting the problem, early, will ensure the best outcome. First, you explain your symptoms to your doctor, who will then need to examine you in person—a phone call is not sufficient. The doctor will perform tests to identify the source and cause, make a diagnosis, and, finally prescribe appropriate treatment.

An ailing business is no different. When warning signs are apparent, your business is telling you that something in its system is wrong. If you want the best outcome, you cannot merely shrug it off as a consequence of an imperfect world, or it will make matters worse. The first thing you need to do is call a business turnaround "doctor" (a specialist or outside accountant), who will examine your financial records and other systems in person, because this also cannot be accomplished with a phone call. In most cases, although the source may be elsewhere, the cause will likely be found in the business's central nervous system—its accounting records. If records are lacking or incomplete, the turnaround professional's ability to diagnose the issue is impeded, and it becomes much more difficult and time consuming to prescribe treatment, while the health of the business continues to erode.

Four major steps to rebuild and re-engage in growth:

- **Recognition of the Problem**

- **Definition of Corrective Action**

- **Remediation**

- **Growth Process**

Although a company may avert a complete failure by taking specific strategic measures—workouts, bankruptcies, receiverships, and sometimes just some old-fashioned belt-tightening—the turnaround process is never natural, or easy. For the troubled business without healthy systems in place, the process is even worse. Fixing accounting weaknesses is imperative because it will mean the difference between a fresh start or a total loss.

The Accountant

Accountants contribute more to a business's success than most people realize. In recent years, the role of the finance professional has evolved from a backroom function—working with numbers—to that of a business partner who can also identify opportunities and solve business problems. Of course, accountants *are* ultimately responsible for numbers, but good ones will know how to interpret what those numbers mean to the business and can also provide strategic guidance, particularly when the health of a business is in jeopardy.

An experienced turnaround accountant is an objective problem solver who can evaluate records, systems, and operations to help identify the exact problem—more quickly than you or your staff—because he or she knows what to look for. A turnaround accountant has worked with troubled businesses before and may even have experience in your industry or something similar. Furthermore, if a company's financial records are not in order or are not accurate, this specialized accountant can direct appropriate measures to correct weak systems, which is always necessary for moving forward.

The value of a savvy accountant, up-to-date systems, and timely reporting is essential in good times. But in a turnaround situation, they are critical. The best accountant for a troubled company is one who can look at the business with a fresh pair of eyes and who has a deep and broad portfolio of turnaround experience for the company to leverage.

Accounting Systems

Of the thousands of bankruptcies and business profitability problems I have encountered over decades as a certified public accountant and turnaround specialist, two commonalities typically arise through the vast majority of them. The first is that the business has poor or inadequate accounting and financial reporting systems, and the second is that the person in charge frequently fails to recognize their value and necessity. These issues go hand in hand.

It is unreasonable to expect any business to operate successfully and profitably for any period without accurate accounting data and the appropriate systems that provide it. Comprehensive and effective accounting systems are an absolute necessity for any business, troubled or not, and these systems are mostly the same for both.

An appropriate accounting system will vary according to both the nature and size of the business. For instance, an accounting system for a hospital will not be the same as for a manufacturing company. Similarly, the system requirements for a small business will vary from those of a large business. But the salient factors are certain. The system must (1) *adequately* support management's reporting requirements and (2) produce them in a *timely* manner.

Integral to the basic hardware and software of the accounting system is the total cost of the support function—human resources. Far too frequently I've seen cost used as the scapegoat for a mediocre accounting system with minimal support. How often have you said, heard, or just thought, "I can't do that. It would cost way too much?" To this, I have two responses: The first is, "You don't know how much it costs you *not* to do it," and the second is, "Your more successful competitors *are* doing it, and if you don't, they'll put you out of business."

Unfortunately, this latter scenario is what happens in many failing businesses. Fortunately, it is entirely possible to turn this around. When management fully recognizes the need to improve systems and staffing and can implement changes, growth typically follows. When management cannot or does not, it may be beyond repair.

Today's technology provides tremendous capabilities in communication, information processing, and almost everything else we touch, see, and do. Any company that doesn't recognize this and apply it to every facet of its business systems is doomed to be left behind. Still, many businesses respond with a Band-Aid approach: upgrading computers and related software, while reducing staff to offset costs. The net effect of "the patch" is typically a higher volume of data processed at the same equivalent cost but with a minimal enhancement to management reporting information. The better approach is to determine which management reporting software, systems, and personnel are necessary to support competitive and viable business operations, then invest in implementing and moving forward.

When accounting systems and related support are viewed principally as a cost, rather than an information center that provides key data for growth, competitiveness, and profitability, it often leads to other adverse decisions. I can think of no better example of this than an apparel manufacturing and distribution company that I was called in to help. The company refused to recognize the necessity of investing in the latest systems to coordinate customer demand, manufacturing, and inventory. Their excuses were textbook. The cost was too high. They needed their cash to support business growth. They could get by with the gradual, patch-work system changes they were making. Eventually, this short-sighted decision making took its toll. Their inventory continued to expand with substantial write-offs, their operating losses persisted, credit lines were restricted, and as the entire industry changed, it left them floundering.

Accounting systems have come a long, long, way since the manually produced Excel spreadsheets. Successful businesses understand the need for the most up-to-date systems and adequate staffing. Companies on the brink of financial distress cannot afford to skimp on these investments, and if they are serious about recovering, they should take immediate steps to correct their course.

Timely Reporting

The second primary element necessary for adequate accounting is that it must be *timely*. Quarterly and, even worse, annual financial statements are meaningless for managing a business. These are meant only for banks and public companies to satisfy their regulatory requirements. For most businesses, monthly financial statements are an absolute must, and these should be available no later than three weeks after the end of each month. Compare these monthly statements to forecasts, budgets, and other operating data, and supplement them during the month with the weekly customer order, sales, production, and other critical reports which are necessary for management to monitor and control business operations.

Business operating and profitability problems rarely happen overnight. Occasionally they might but, generally, those that pop up quickly, such as fire, theft, product liability, and natural disasters, are insurable. In the distressed business, problems typically grow over a period and result from things such as market deterioration, product line erosion, changing technology, bad management decisions, capital deficits, and similar issues. Even these latter problems are to a great extent "insurable" through proper management attention and action. As long as management and business owners pay attention to this information, management can identify and deal with issues *as they occur* with the necessary systems in place to deliver timely reports.

I am continually amazed by the number of times I'm introduced to troubled companies that have been losing money, not just a few months but for years, and have not taken any substantive corrective action. Equally bad, if not worse, are the companies that were unknowingly losing money but were reporting profitability because of their inadequate accounting systems and controls. The attitude of many of these business owners was frequently to ignore the problems with the unadmitted hope that they would miraculously correct themselves and go away—everything would turn out all right in the end. This attitude is particularly common in established businesses that have served their markets for years and become complacent. They frequently rely on the same business traditions, the same sales and operation information, and the same business practices that they have used without considerable change. Then one day, they wake up when it far too late, and find that they will possibly lose their businesses.

The very first principal of turning around a financially distressed business is to recognize that a problem exists. Issues usually evolve gradually, before the negative impact is felt. Consequently, resolving issues also takes time, and that is why maintaining effective and timely accounting and management reporting systems, including the continuous and routine review of financial information by management and business owners, is critical.

Failing companies routinely forego timely financial reporting, generate few, if any, meaningful management reports, and don't place a very high value on up-to-date accounting systems and sufficient support staff. By the time the impact of these poor decisions is recognized, the resultant damage is so severe that recovery is frequently impossible. There is no one magical system to address all issues for all companies. The nature and size of the business will determine the appropriate system. What all have in common, however, is timely reporting and sharing the necessary information.

Financial Statements

Foremost, an adequate accounting system generates monthly financial statements. The emphasis here is on monthly—not quarterly, annually, or whenever the accountant gets around to it. Monthly. At a minimum, this includes balance sheets and income statements generated no later than the end of the third week following each month end. (Please don't think lightly of this seemingly obvious comment, because you might be surprised how few businesses truly accomplish this and commit to it as a fundamental policy of their business operations!)

Aside from basic financial statements, the most useful report is an annual profit and loss forecast. Rarely is this report found in a financially troubled business. The P&L forecast should be integrated with the monthly financial reporting process to compare current month and year-to-date operating results. Such reporting is the only way to effectively monitor operating performance during the year in order to timely identify problems as they occur and manage the business to meet planned objectives. The P&L forecast is one of the most meaningful and productive reports for directing successful operations, and it is also almost universally absent from the offices of any financially troubled business.

Think about this for just a millisecond: One of the first steps taken when driving to a new destination is to check the route to know where to go and the best way to get there. Likewise, for any construction project, the architect and builder will prepare plans so that the project can be completed to correct specifications and design. Why then does the business owner believe that the business can be managed and grown without forecasts, budgets, and plans? This, however, is not uncommon among many business owners. All successful companies have plans that require meaningful financial statements and reports, while the problems of many failing businesses can be attributed, at least to some extent, to their absence.

Management Information Systems

Beyond basic financial statements and forecasts, systems should account for the unique business characteristics and the information needed to support those operations, also known as management information systems. These can cover a broad range of support functions, but some of the most common include

- Inventory management and control,

- Sales reports,

- Gross profit and product-line profitability, and

- Operation support systems such as manufacturing, distribution, scheduling, and other specific control systems.

- Identifying these systems begins with three simple questions:

- What are the most critical elements of profitability and control of the business operations?

- What information management systems are in place to support these?

- How efficiently are they operating?

It is astounding how frequently businesses attempt to operate without information management systems to support fundamental operations. Or, if they exist, systems that are inefficient and inadequate. For financially troubled businesses this is almost always the case.

Systems that adequately support operations offer many foundational management benefits and building blocks, such as accounting, planning, forecasting, and analysis. In many businesses, management information systems also play an essential role in monitoring marketplace conditions, customer sentiments, and even competition. Where management information infrastructure is not in place, nothing happens—at least nothing that you want to happen—and in an increasingly data-driven economy, the cost of inadequate or unavailable information can be significant. Business owners who recognize this fact and maintain appropriate management information systems operate more efficiently and more profitably, and are generally among the leaders in their industries. Those who fail to recognize this fact are among the least profitable and weakest performers with very shortened lifespans.

For example, I have seen far too many manufacturing companies attempt to operate without adequate systems to control and coordinate the purchasing and manufacturing of raw materials with customer demand. The same holds true for distribution businesses, only without the complexity of the actual manufacturing process. Without these information systems, the entire business process can be faulty: from ordering inventory and materials on the front end, to the manufacturing and/or warehousing in the middle, to the availability of goods to meet customer orders and delivery requirements at the end. As a result, businesses compensate for these deficiencies by ordering too much on the front end, enduring far too much inefficiency in the middle, and holding too much inventory on the back end, which is disproportionate to customer demand.

More precisely, when a business is experiencing difficulties, management information systems make their inner workings visible. They enable the turnaround consultant to isolate problem areas and recommend corrective actions. When they are nonexistent or inadequate, the consultant will recommend that such systems be implemented immediately to monitor and control the turnaround process. Without management systems in place, the turnaround is much more difficult and is often not feasible.

The Business Owner

Most business owners are familiar with the garden-variety challenges that crop up during the ordinary course of operations. But for owners of companies in financial distress, the challenges become unique. Problems have likely accumulated over a period of time and surfaced without ever coming to the owner's attention. When this occurs, the company has at least three primary hurdles to overcome and affect a turnaround process.

The first hurdle is usually the toughest: to accept that somewhere along the line faulty, ingrained business practices developed under the owner's management. If an owner cannot recognize his or her role in the root of the failing business, he or she is even less capable of taking necessary corrective actions.

The distressed business owner is often inclined to blame others. The object of that blame may be specific persons inside the organization, or it may be outside forces, such as changes in cultural attitudes, technology, market conditions, business practices, demographics, or whatever. In any case, the problems occurred under the owner's stewardship, and he or she is at fault for failing to catch and resolve them promptly. In other words, the owner must admit responsibility, because blaming others or outside forces will only make matters worse.

The second hurdle is to accept that the problems have most likely been gathering over time, and that corrective actions also require time and patience. Because problems haven't occurred overnight, curing them won't either. Steps to replace systems, change personnel, or recapitalize the business, if required, all take time. Such decisions are not easy to make, and the process of implementing them can be complicated, not to mention that money necessary to fund corrective actions may be hard to obtain for the financially challenged business.

It is critical for the business owner to accept that *everything* in a turnaround takes time, patience, and planning. If any of it were quick and easy, there wouldn't have been problems in the first place. Without such acknowledgment, the entire turnaround process is doomed to fail.

The third major hurdle for the business owner is to accept that remedies often require significant changes at the foundational level, and this cannot be done alone. Whether the cause of problems was lack of oversight, inadequate systems, or inability to adapt, it is the rare owner or CEO who can fix the problems he or she created. To succeed in a turnaround, the business owner must turn over some or all control to those who specialize in turnaround situations. These professionals are more experienced, objective, and capable of doing what needs to be done.

Based on my own experience in managing and operating many companies through the turnaround process, I have had almost universal success when the business owner placed me in a position of complete control over the business's operations. Conversely, when I merely acted in the capacity of consultant, having to convince the business owner to change personal beliefs and practices, I rarely experienced any satisfactory level of success. While it is fair to question whether my ability to influence others is lacking, almost all other professionals in my field claim similar experiences. In a distressed business turn-around, a business owner's best interest is to allow the specialists to do their jobs by giving them control.

The Successful Turnaround

Indeed, individual company owners with natural talent have stumbled onto critical products or revolutionary technology and have achieved success with little apparent difficulty. But the business graveyards are also full of similar enterprises that have failed. Bill Gates didn't realize his success with Microsoft by accident. All businesses can and usually do have their inherent difficulties and problems to overcome during their development cycles. Some succeed, while others fall by the wayside. Still, other enterprising individuals turn over their ideas and businesses to professional managers, who can drive a successful future.

But one reality exists. No matter how large or small, commonplace or revolutionary, if your business is losing money, can't pay its debts, or break even, it is trying to tell you that something is systemically wrong. You cannot merely shrug that off as a consequence of an imperfect world. You need to take key steps to turn it around.

The business that successfully accomplishes a turnaround will first and foremost continue to reliably deliver the product or service it provides, to the best of its ability. It will engage the appropriate professionals to examine, diagnose, and prescribe treatment. It will ensure that accounting and operational systems provide accurate management and financial information on a timely basis, enough to turn it around. And, perhaps most critical, the business owner or owners will be open to change and willing to facilitate the process.

Turning around the underperforming business rarely comes easy. A company will get plenty of warning signals before demise is inevitable. The observant business owner will act promptly to seek help and set forth a plan for recovery. To do so can mean the difference between a fresh start or a total loss.

Samuel R. Biggs is the lead partner of SLBiggs, a division of SingerLewak. Mr. Biggs has over 40 years of diversified experience in public accounting and private industry in the areas of financial management and planning, M&A, corporate reorganization, insolvency, and commercial business services. He has worked extensively with troubled companies in financial reorganization, creditor workouts, and insolvency. As a former bankruptcy trustee in the Central District of California, Mr. Biggs was responsible for the administration of over 12,000 bankruptcy cases, many of which were businesses he managed and operated through the reorganization process. Contact him at sbiggs@slbiggs.com.

6

Debt Financing for the Insolvent Company

LAWRENCE N. HURWITZ

Going deep into business debt can be a stressful and harrowing experience. When combined with plunging sales and profits, it can be an omen of bankruptcy—a business's worst nightmare. Filing for bankruptcy doesn't always mean the end of a company's run. In fact, for some, it is an opportunity for a fresh start.

When the leading manufacturer of specialty coated paper—used in magazines and catalogs—was battered by a confluence of external factors as publishers turned to online channels, the company experienced an accelerated and unprecedented decline. It had accumulated substantial debt on which it was required to pay annual interest, leaving only a long-shot chance to restructure successfully.

But the company didn't want to quit. Its advisors went to work constructing a pre-chapter 11 bankruptcy plan that would leverage the confidence of its incumbent lenders, new investors, and creditors. Their work paid off. Less than six months after filing chapter 11, the manufacturer was able to convert a significant portion of its liabilities into equity and emerge as a reorganized entity, and a much stronger company.

— ◇ —

The troubled or insolvent business must regain a solid financial footing. Whether a company's restructuring involves a court-related transaction—chapter 11 bankruptcy—or an out-of-court settlement, some financing will be needed to stabilize the company. But funding for the insolvent or troubled company is never a sure thing, nor easy. Among only a few available options, debt financing is the likely place to start.

Debt financing includes both secured and unsecured loans—although few, if any, will be based on your name or reputation, or on an idea alone. Most lenders require physical security in the form of collateral. If the debtor defaults, that collateral is forfeited to satisfy payment of the debt. While this may seem straightforward, rarely is that the case.

Collateral Analysis

The asset analysis is the cornerstone of any bankruptcy proceeding, and the practical and strategic implications of valuation play key roles throughout the entire bankruptcy process. Every constituent party in the restructuring process will make decisions based on the value of the debtor and its assets.

To obtain financing or capital, the debtor will try to use some or all of its assets as collateral. Commonsense logic would be that the more valuable the guarantee, the more funding the company can borrow. But it's not that simple. Lenders and investors are looking for and looking at a wide variety of factors—no small task. Collateral assets are multi-layered and complicated by the diverse nature of lenders and investors. That's why a company in distress will need a collateral analysis.

In arranging new financing, the insolvent company's first consideration is to assess the *type* and *value* of the collateral that it can offer a lender. (Keep in mind that a lender will always evaluate collateral assets in a "worst case" scenario to mitigate its risks.) Due to the uncertainty of outcome, it is scarce for an insolvent company to obtain financing without attractive collateral.

The lender will request, and the company must facilitate and pay for, appraisals and other types of valuations. Lenders typically require valuations in two formats: NOLV (net orderly liquidation value) and FLV (forced liquidation value or "quick liq"). In situations which seem to have a high probability of emerging from distress or readily saleable inventory is, many lenders will accept NOLV due to the likelihood that any foreclosure will provide adequate time for an orderly disposition (usually within six months). However, when the lender lacks confidence in the borrower and the inventory is more problematic (e.g., perishables), the lender will use the FLV valuation to obtain the highest recovery.

The lender will also consider the likelihood of the company's emerging from bankruptcy in structuring the loan. The less likely that the company can emerge from bankruptcy, the less likely that the company can attract debt capital. Some lenders may be willing to do "DIP" loans, i.e., debtor in possession loans to companies that are in chapter 11 reorganization, with the expectation that they will emerge successfully from bankruptcy. Other lenders may structure their loans as "exit financing," and condition their loans on the debtor's exiting the chapter 11.

The following information breaks down *lendable assets* commonly associated with both bankruptcies and out-of-court restructurings. Investors, asset purchasers, or merger partners will also look for the same in an asset analysis.

Accounts Receivable

The most valuable assets to a lender are fungible or self-liquidating, such as money owed to the business. In an insolvency situation, the most accessible fungible asset to collateralize, barring a few caveats, is accounts receivable.

The lender will evaluate accounts receivable collateral using these primary metrics:

1. **The concentration of debtors.** Is there one predominant customer versus numerous entities doing business with the firm?
2. **The current status of aging receivables.** What percentage is 30 days or fewer versus 90 days or more past due?
3. **Quality and quantity of customer base.** Are the company's customers mostly Fortune 500 firms with significant receivables, or numerous lesser-known companies with very small invoices due?
4. **The longevity of customer history.** Are these long-time customers or recently acquired accounts?
5. **Progress billing or pre-billing status.** Are all invoices issued after goods and services are delivered or is there progress billing or pre-billing, also known as milestone billing, in place?
6. **The certainty of payment.** Is there a significant measure of confidence that debtors will still pay in a liquidation scenario?
7. **Retention/return conditions for the collateral base.** Are there customers with the right to return goods for credit?

If so, would this deplete available borrowing off the receivables?

The method of payment for receivables is also a significant consideration in financing receivables. Most lenders will require a "lockbox" arrangement that can only be accessed by the lender, with customers remitting payments to a specific account. After the lender's lockbox receives funds, the lender will make its charges against those funds for any agreed-to interest and fees, apply the balance of the proceeds to the loan, and then advance the remaining proceeds to the borrower, usually as part of a "revolving" loan. In industries in which cash payments are made directly to the seller, this scenario can impede the ability to borrow on receivables.

Practical Pointer: Creditors continue to collect receivables despite insolvency in an average liquidation. Therefore, more lenders are active in this space than in any other. The distressed owner must maintain close control over its receivables to protect collateral values with daily monitoring and an explicit focus on collections. If management gets distracted and loses control over its receivables, the ability to obtain debt financing will be much more difficult.

Inventory

A company's inventory is often considered a liquid asset. But liquidation values can be difficult to ascertain, and in the event of default, lenders will want quick access to loan repayment. Therefore, lenders scrutinize inventory, using the following considerations:

1. **How current is the inventory?** Products that will sell quickly are considered more valuable than items that will take a long time to find a buyer.
2. **Are the goods branded or licensed?** Branded or licensed inventory may require permission from the licensor before being sold into the market. Depending on how complicated that might be, it can increase or decrease their value.
3. **What is the nature of inventory?** If the stock is blank T-shirts, it will likely have many potential buyers. On the other hand, if the inventory is highly sophisticated electronics, it may have few ready buyers, if any.
4. **What is the condition and status of inventory?** Lenders place a greater value on goods when a perpetual inventory system is in place *and* the goods are in excellent condition.
5. **Is inventory manufactured and shipped from abroad?** Inventory that has not yet been received by the borrower has a lower value. Lenders are often reluctant to advance funds for collateral inventory manufactured and shipped from abroad.

Inventory of raw materials or finished goods is usually the most desirable to lenders. On the other hand, work-in-progress inventory (WIP)—products that are at various stages of the production process—can be problematic, as assessing value is more difficult, and therefore considered less attractive collateral for third parties. Accounting for WIP varies from company to company, and one company's WIP may not be entirely comparable to another's. Allocation of WIP overhead based on human labor is different than that of machine hours.

Machinery and Equipment (Fixed Assets)

Fixed assets—machinery and equipment—are less liquid, but are easier to value than inventory, with one exception: lenders are keenly aware that the book value of equipment on the company's balance sheet may not accurately reflect actual liquidation value. An example is when a company has used accelerated depreciation for tax purposes. In such cases, fixed assets may be worth considerably more than the books reflect. Conversely, if the company's machinery and equipment is soon to become obsolete, the book value may overstate collateral value.

Likewise, some lenders will look at items such as vehicles—rolling stock—and value them based on wear and tear. The actual value, based upon such depreciation, is often a lot less than the company's assumed value of these assets.

Finally, the lender will want to know what a probable auction realization will be in the event of default. As auctioneers often own appraisal firms, their services will be used to estimate collateral value in a default scenario. The final loan amount includes the appraisal cost.

Real Estate

If the borrower owns real estate, the lender will want to know that the property can be sold quickly to a third party and, therefore, its value is based on a use case—its use to a potential buyer. The most favorable real estate is multi-use buildings and land.

Well maintained multi-use buildings typically receive the highest value, as these can be economically re-purposed for a broad variety of future occupants. Conversely, single-use buildings, such as refrigerated warehouses in highly restricted zoning areas, are not as quickly disposed of and hold less immediate liquidation value for the lender.

Furthermore, if a property is found to have environmental contamination concerns, it may be considered more of a liability than an asset.

Intellectual Property

A borrower can use brand names, patents, trademarks, and other intellectual property as loan collateral. Where they exist, the lender will require an opinion on prospective licensing opportunities. Although intellectual property is commonly considered a complicated collateral asset, its value can be quite significant. Sharper Image is an example of a famous brand name that became more valuable in licensing, even after the operating entity was no longer in business. When the company became defunct, many buyers were interested in purchasing the name to place on other products.

Patents are more problematic. The nature of the owner's business determines their value. If the patent is extremely valuable, there will be buyers in the event of default, and it will carry significant collateral value for the lender. But if a patent is relatively unproven or unclear in its purpose, or its value is unascertained, it will hold little value in a liquidation.

Management Expertise and Reputation

Management expertise, company reputation, and customer and employee loyalty—"goodwill"—can hold collateral value for the distressed business. Although goodwill is an intangible and usually worthless in liquidation, it can be attractive to lenders if there are prospective merger candidates that would jump at a chance to expand with a ready-made market opportunity.

Recurring Revenues and Subscriptions

Business models that include recurring revenue streams and subscriptions, such as those found in companies that provide software, contract maintenance, or cloud-based applications, can hold significant collateral value. However, lenders must be confident that the disclosure of insolvency to the customer base will not interrupt the continuity of payment for these services.

In attempting to present recurring revenues and subscriptions as collateral, the company would need to produce solid records and, possibly, projections regarding competition and market outlook.

Finding Financing

Once collateral values are estimated, the insolvent company is ready to seek out a source of financing. Almost every business will have previous experience borrowing money, but as a struggling company, it will be charting new territory. In debt financing finding the right fit is critical. To do so usually requires experience and connections, time and patience, and often the services of a turnaround specialist.

Although the distressed company may have limited options for sources of financing, lender liquidity, expertise, and "certainty" should be factored into the borrower's decision. For example, a lender with an extensive track record in financing other insolvencies will likely influence not only the speed and efficiency of the process but also the certainty of closing. And because time is usually of the essence, the distressed borrower will want to be reasonably confident that the loan will close promptly.

Existing Lender

The first and best option for the distressed company is to approach the existing lender. The incumbent lender is likely familiar with the assets and prospects of the borrower. And unless there is suspicion of bad faith, the current lender has significant motivation to ensure that the company has adequate capital to operate for at least two reasons: First, if the company deteriorates further, this increasingly impairs the ability of the lender to get paid and, as a result, if the company liquidates, the lender may be forced to take a more extensive write-down on its loan. Second, if the company files a chapter 11, there is a risk that the lender may be "primed." Priming in chapter 11 involves a court order which involuntarily subordinates the old lender to any new source of capital, and may impair the original lender's ability to collect on that debt.

For example, if the incumbent lender declines to provide continuing financing to the distressed entity, the borrower may have no choice but to approach a new lender. Typically, new lenders will not agree to finance a company in chapter 11 without the security of a first-priority lien. Accordingly, unless there are unused collateral assets with the existing lender, the insolvent company may, in certain circumstances, apply to the bankruptcy court to "prime" the existing lender. Priming grants the new lender a senior lien on the very same assets that were used to collateralize the current lender.

To be sure, obtaining a court order for a "priming" loan is not easily accomplished, as the bankruptcy law usually respects the validity and priority of the existing lender's lien. However, if the borrower can show that the current lender is "adequately protected," then the court may grant a priming order. The argument for adequate protection can be made by showing financial projections in which a new senior lender advances funds (which the existing lender refuses to do) and positively monetizes existing assets. For example, if a new lender advances money for completion of raw materials into inventory, for which there is a ready buyer, assets that might otherwise fetch only liquidation value can be sold at a markup, protecting both the new and existing lenders.

Other Lenders

Financing through a regulated entity, such as an FDIC-insured bank, will typically be the least costly for the borrower but is often not available for the distressed business due to rigorous government controls placed on regulated lenders, such as commercial banks. If a governmental agency regulates the incumbent lender, such lender is required by law to reserve an estimate of loss in the event of foreclosure. Regulated lenders, for the most part, are more conservative than non-regulated lenders.

The bank must write down the value of any such loan to an amount of assumed recovery. The effect of such reserve amount has two possible outcomes: The bank is anxious to get the loan off its books and will take the best offer. In this case, the lender may, for example, be willing to sell off its loan for a steep discount. Or, the bank seeks some repatriation of the reserve amount (i.e., a recovered amount more significant than the written down amount), in which case the lender may be more cooperative with the borrower, seeking to assist in improving its operations. The regulated lender's actions in a workout sometimes turn on the specific situation of the bank (e.g., the regulators may be pressuring the bank to get rid of its bad loans quickly).

Accordingly, as a borrower, it can be challenging to understand the driving forces motivating a regulated lender's actions in a loan restructuring. If the company's current lender declines or another commercially regulated lender is not viable, there are two options: Find a comprehensive lender that will consider all types of collateral or work with several specialized sources.

The comprehensive or all-inclusive lender, which will consider all types of collateral, is ultimately the most versatile choice. If that option is not available, the borrower may pursue multiple, specialized lenders that will have a "sweet spot," or preference for certain types of collateral. Some lenders will only finance accounts receivable, while others will specialize in fixed assets, real estate, or inventory. Still others may be looking for assets in a particular industry or geographic footprint or may focus solely on intangible collateral, such as intellectual property and goodwill.

For example, a company that owns mining equipment might seek out a lender who is experienced in the type of collateral found within the industry and can facilitate the most aggressive loan profile. When a company owns a famous brand name or a patent that brings in recurring royalty income, seeking out a lender that specializes in intangibles will be optimal. Examples of successful brand name loans include BUM Equipment, Twinkies, Sharper Image, and Fuller Brush.

Financing with multiple lenders does, however, become more complicated. For example, all participants must agree to an "inter-creditor" arrangement as part of the restructuring process. The inter-creditor agreement spells out the rights of each lender and the collateral it holds, and also addresses the order in which each lender is entitled to exercise its rights if there is a default. Without such agreement, it could become difficult to determine which lender has rights to which assets in the event of default. For example, when one lender is collateralized by inventory and another by accounts receivable, the collateral becomes a moving target because all inventory sold on credit morphs into accounts receivable.

In cases in which there is adequate asset coverage, the best choice may be a commercial finance operator that will lend only a percentage of liquidation values. These asset-based lenders, often termed ABL lenders, will use a formula to determine how much they will loan. Formulas are usually 80 percent on accounts receivable and 50 percent on other assets. For example, for every $1 million in receivables, the borrower can expect to receive up to $800,000 in loan advances. This variety of lender is often cheaper than a "hard money" source, but more expensive than a bank.

Other sources of capital for the distressed or bankrupt borrower will depend upon the profile of those most likely to fit the company. Some distressed borrowers choose to work with so-called hard money lenders, also known as "loan to own." Hard money lenders do not focus on the rehabilitation of the company. They merely scrutinize the hard assets to ensure that they get their money back in a worst-case scenario. Lenders that provide hard money are expensive, and working with them can be difficult. Unregulated private investors or companies at higher interest rates than conventional commercial loans commonly issue hard-money loans.

Alternately, the borrower might approach a strategic competitor or a company that is interested in getting involved in the borrower's industry. Such arrangements are often user-friendly, but run the risk of the borrower's ultimately losing control of the company.

The next option is to identify a strategic partner that may be interested in getting involved with a debtor. For example, in one particular case, an insolvent retail chain was unable to get credit from its suppliers but found a manufacturing partner that had substantial excess inventory. The manufacturer entered a partnership agreement, contributing merchandise to the retailer's outlets. The money generated by the sale of these goods was used to finance the business and in exchange, the manufacturer received an equity stake in the company.

Of course, there are also money sources such as hedge funds, family offices, and private individuals that may be interested in the lending opportunity if they consider repayment a high probability.

Yet another option is for the company's owners to put more of their own money or assets into the business to keep it going. Unfortunately, in many cases, the principals have already exhausted their assets before the insolvency and, therefore, this option is not practical.

Family and friends are sometimes willing and able to invest, and this could be a very viable and cost-effective way to obtain necessary capital. Of course, if that source is already tapped out, the door is closed.

Approaching Capital Sources

Experienced and qualified advisors such as a turnaround consultant or a chief restructuring officer, known as a CRO, are often essential to producing a good result in financing and related decision-making. In the majority of insolvencies, the company's principals have limited experience in distress financing. Consequently, engaging the right advisors, who can objectively assess the situation and provide viable options, is prudent.

Because most companies wait until the last minute to acknowledge that the business is financially troubled, filing for bankruptcy becomes a time-sensitive situation. Therefore, the worst thing a distressed company can do is enter a blind alley. The company's turnaround team should include an experienced financial advisor who can find the most appropriate lender via the most direct means.

For example, if a $20 million financing is needed, there are a limited number of lenders able to make this much money available. The advisors will know who they are. Perhaps most critical, the advisor can guide the borrower away from lenders who will ultimately fail to perform or know the composition of a lender's portfolio. If a lender does not include experience in the company's industry, the advisor can quickly determine its actual interest in speaking with the borrower.

Experienced advisors can also assist in negotiating with parties to strike the most favorable terms for the borrower. They will know which lender is most appropriate for the borrower's situation and what the conventional pricing matrix should be.

While finding money for a firm in financial distress can be intimidating, using the right team to assist in the process can make all the difference. Knowing the right places to look for debt financing can be invaluable.

Preparation

Before the borrower approaches a lender, adequate preparation is necessary. However, while trying to keep the business running under duress, the management team often becomes overwhelmed with the demands of handling the restructuring process. Engaging a skilled turnaround consultant or CRO in the early stage can relieve management of the most onerous burden and move the financing effort forward effectively.

Although the company will feel the adviser's value throughout the entire operation, where debt financing is concerned, his or her primary role will be to prepare the required lender documentation—the package. The adviser will also present the borrower's case to the potential lender or provider of capital.

Nearly every funding source a distressed company approaches will have a checklist of required information. This package may include

- The amount of funding requested and over what period

- The use of the funding

- The borrower's books and records

- Are accounts receivable current?

- Is the inventory controlled by a perpetual system?

- Does the borrower's infrastructure maintain a system to produce reliable and detailed financial reports on a continuing, current basis?

- Proof of the quality and commitment of management and employees

- Collateral documentation and supplemental securities, such as guarantees of the principals

- Detailed projections

- Confirmation that licenses and taxes up to date

Because the lender is looking for borrowers who can be depended upon to keep the creditors well informed on an ongoing basis, the borrowing request package must be complete and appropriate. Commonly, deals that present incomplete and/or inaccurate information to the lender in the first approach fail. The experienced adviser will present the borrower to the lender in the best possible light.

The important takeaway for the distressed business is to understand that insolvency doesn't mean that all is lost. There are several ways for a company to obtain the funding needed to stabilize and re-emerge. A chapter 11 bankruptcy may be a public relations challenge, the process may be intimidating and may require an army of advisors, but it also gives ownership breathing room to refocus, restructure, *and* refinance.

Financing for a distressed entity is an extremely complex undertaking, but many companies do find better terms and can emerge from bankruptcy with less debt, new capital, and a fresh outlook for better days ahead.

— ◇ —

Lawrence N. Hurwitz is Founding Chairman of Lawrence Financial Group in Los Angeles. He started the investment banking company in 1990 to provide financial services to middle-market companies seeking funding for growth and/or restructuring. In its 28 years, the firm has made billions of dollars of capital available to more than 1,500 firms nationwide.

Mr. Hurwitz began his career as an investment banker on Wall Street subsequent to his receipt of MBA with Distinction from Harvard University Graduate School of Business Administration. He ultimately became CEO of a New York Stock Exchange member broker/dealer prior to moving to Los Angeles.

A native of Austin, Texas, and an undergraduate at the University of Texas at Austin, Mr. Hurwitz has two children and two grandchildren. He also serves as Chairman Emeritus of Woodbury University in Burbank, California. Contact him at <u>Lnhurwitz@Lawrencefinancial.com</u>.

7

Valuation Issues for Distressed Businesses

By Nevin Sanli and Henry Kaskov

For many business owners, cash flow management can be the most rewarding *or* the most daunting part of daily operations. During high-growth and profitable stages of a company's life cycle, looking at a business's bank statements and balance sheet can excite and motivate owners to open the doors each morning. Conversely, weathering periods of slow growth and diminishing profits is dispiriting. But when a business reaches a state at which it is no longer able to meet its financial obligations to lenders, insurers, vendors, or even employees, the prospect of bankruptcy becomes all too real.

The distressed financial position can be a temporary setback, or something more ominous. Even seemingly healthy businesses in robust industries can experience increased competition or market obsolescence, or get caught in regulatory changes, which when combined with an inability to adapt, leave little room for recovery.

Among the most dreaded event in the life of a business is a date with any one or more of the "Three Deadly Ls"—loss of customers, lawsuits, or loading up on debt. They are the harbinger of almost sure mortality.

— ◇ —

Three Deadly Ls

Loss of customers. Acquiring new customers and cultivating repeat patronage are the lifeblood of successful businesses, while losing customers can be an omen of impending insolvency. Take, for example, Ann Arbor, Michigan-based Borders Group, Inc., which was one of the largest international book and music retailers before its dissolution.

Borders, a 40-year old mega-bookstore chain with over 650 stores at its peak, could not curb a years-long trend of decreasing customer traffic. Outside forces, including increased competition from Amazon, Barnes & Noble, and even Wal-Mart, coupled with shifting consumer preferences for electronic books and e-readers, hampered in-store traffic and revenue. Although Borders eventually launched proprietary e-readers—the Kobo and Cruz—it was too little and too late. Despite heavy promotion, consumers continued to choose its competitors' products, further eroding the company's financial position. Subsequently, executive and management turnover ultimately forced the company into bankruptcy, and in 2011 the company closed all its stores.

Lawsuit. A lawsuit can have a sudden and drastic impact on a business and its operations. In early 2014, Gawker, an online news and gossip website, published portions of a sex tape of Terry Gene Bollea, aka former pro wrestler Hulk Hogan, who then sued Gawker for an invasion of privacy. A jury sided with Mr. Bollea, awarding damages of $140 million, based on the profits and an increased value obtained by Gawker from publishing the story. This verdict not only forced the company to declare bankruptcy, but Nick Denton, Gawker's founder and a listed defendant, had to declare personal bankruptcy as well.

Following the Gawker bankruptcy, Univision Communications purchased Gawker Media and its other web properties, including the sports site, Deadspin; the tech blog, Gizmodo; and, the news and gossip site, Jezebel, for $135 million at auction. Gawker.com, the flagship website, was shut down completely.

Loading up on debt. Managing debt is critical to maintaining a successful business. Interest and principal payments can have a crimping impact on cash flow and reduce a business's ability to expand or innovate, as was experienced by Sports Authority. Once the largest sporting goods retailer in the United States, Sports Authority was purchased for $1.3 billion in a leveraged buyout in 2006. Despite being in the athletic apparel industry, which experienced high growth in the years following the buyout, the company's high debt load and interest payments restricted its ability to innovate its in-store experience and expand its online business.

In addition, a multitude of competitive market forces led to declining sales and the shuttering of business operations in 2016. At auction, Dick's Sporting Goods purchased the Sports Authority brand name for $15 million, while Tiger Capital Group, Hilco Global, and Gordon Brothers won the auction for all remaining stores and liquidation. The bid was 101 percent of the original cost of the stores' inventory, plus $1.8 million.

Duration of Financial Distress

The degree to which a business suffers from one of the deadly Ls can range from a temporary setback to a major restructuring or bankruptcy. Management's ability to recognize a potential threat to the business's cash flow and assets and to implement a plan to withstand a financial blow can be the difference between a bad quarter and a full-fledged failure of the firm.

The experiences of Borders, Gawker, and Sports Authority are not unique and can befall businesses of any size and within any industry. Statistically, the majority of all bankruptcies in the U.S. were small businesses with revenues of less than $2.5 million. Companies with revenues between $2.5 million and $1 billion comprised 20 percent of all bankruptcies, while service businesses and those in the finance/insurance/real estate industries involved approximately 28 percent and 18 percent of total bankruptcies, respectively.

Temporary Impact

When a business approaches or enters a distressed state, creditors become more concerned about the business's ability to make future interest and principal payments. A *cash flow* or *solvency analysis*, prepared by an experienced business appraiser, can provide key information and insight into a business's health, while a *valuation analysis* can determine the fair market value of the business's tangible and intangible assets, which become key assets in any future restructuring.

Such analyses are critical for creditors navigating through a debtor's financial challenges. Creditors need to understand whether the financial distress is a result of a one-time, non-recurring event on the business's cash flow and its ability to continue operations, or if it is a significant, unique event, such as the damage verdict experienced by Gawker, which can deal a fatal blow to business operations.

Although smaller events such as those involving product recall or loss of a key employee (e.g., manager, salesperson, engineer) can negatively impact business, they do not necessarily force a bankruptcy reorganization or liquidation. Therefore, a solvency and cash flow analysis, along with a determination of the *going-concern* and **liquidation values** of assets, will provide creditors with a comprehensive picture of the business's current financial condition and its ability to continue making debt payments, fund ongoing business operations, and raise capital by possibly selling some assets. Additionally, an appraiser can examine vital financial ratios to determine whether, and for how long, the business might not comply with its loan covenants. Understanding this information will affect what action, if any, creditors must take to protect their financial investment in the business.

When a one-time event, such as loss of a key customer or employee, product recall, negative publicity, or other unforeseen temporary development, impacts a company, management has tools at its disposal to ensure continuity of operations and satisfy creditors. For example, payment of payroll expenses and outstanding debt is paramount to the business's ability to continue operations and withstand a significant financial setback, but management must also attempt to work with its vendors to extend payment terms and/or delay non-essential business investments and capital expenditures.

Other remedies might include

- Collecting outstanding receivables to accelerate cash inflows;

- Eliminating nonessential business travel, advertising, entertainment, consulting, and other related expenses, to the extent that cutting programs does not further undercut sales and operations; and

- Reducing ownership compensation and management bonuses to cover cash shortfalls.

Management's ability to make such quick but difficult decisions can determine whether or not it will overcome short-term adversity and avoid bankruptcy.

Restructuring

Unfortunately, some businesses will not be able to withstand the financial impact caused by a one-time event or series of setbacks, and ultimately may be forced to implement significant restructurings to remain in business. Demands of creditors looking to secure and preserve their investments may necessitate layoffs of management and staff; divestiture of divisions, business units, and intellectual property/patents; or a wholesale change in the business model.

A recent example of a large corporate restructuring involves Yahoo!, which at one point was one of the most visited websites and email providers worldwide. Over time, the tech giant experienced decreasing web traffic and competition from other online news and email providers. Along with executive turnover and well-publicized failures to acquire ancillary web properties, the company experienced an unsustainable drop in revenues. Furthermore, multiple hacks of over one billion email accounts eroded the company's public image and trust.

In 2016 the company announced a major restructuring of the business, including employee layoffs, divestitures of business units, and a potential merger or sale of the company. Then CEO Marissa Mayer reportedly prepared an "invest/maintain/kill" list to guide the future of its various business units. Many suspected that the company would look to lower expenses and remove non-profitable business operations in the hopes of finding a buyer for its most valuable assets. Although Mayer managed to triple the company's share price during her five years at the helm, ultimately it was not enough. In June 2017, Yahoo! sold its operations to Verizon Communications for $4.48 billion. It was a devastating loss for a company that once had a market value of $125 billion.

Bankruptcy

If an out-of-court restructuring does not improve operations, a business will likely be forced into a bankruptcy liquidation (chapter 7), bankruptcy reorganization (chapter 11), or an assignment for the benefit of creditors.

The experiences of Borders and Sports Authority are two examples of chapter 7 bankruptcy, which resulted in a liquidation of assets to pay creditors. Chapter 11 bankruptcies, which require reorganization and restructuring of the business, are sometimes the preferred method when equity and debt holders wish to reshape the company and continue business operations.

The airline industry has seen many examples of chapter 11 bankruptcies, led by United Airlines' 38-month process that ended in 2006. Like many rival airlines, United was unable to contain increasing labor and operating costs, causing it to enter bankruptcy protection in December 2002. Following the restructuring, United had approximately 30 percent fewer employees, 20 percent fewer airplanes, and 20 percent lower operating costs than it had before the bankruptcy. The airline also eliminated dozens of unprofitable daily routes. These changes allowed United to successfully stabilize operations and increase profits over the next few years. In 2010, United merged with Continental Holdings to create the world's largest airline carrier at the time. (For a full discussion of chapter 11 bankruptcies, see chapter 1 of this book.)

Another option available to businesses in most states is an Assignment for the Benefit of Creditors, or ABC, which is governed by state law and can be more advantageous to a business. The debtor executes an agreement—usually in the form of a contract or trust agreement—whereby the debtor assigns its right, title, and interest in its assets to a neutral, third-party assignee, in trust for the benefit of its creditors to initiate a general ABC. The assignee then becomes responsible for liquidating the assets and distributing the proceeds to creditors under the state's law repayment priority scheme. ABCs are discussed in greater detail in chapter 9.

Secured and unsecured creditors follow a specific process to file claims and receive distributions of payments. Therefore, unlike a bankruptcy filing, the ABC eliminates the "race to the courthouse" in which creditors of a troubled business often engage. This out-of-court process is typically faster and less expensive than chapter 7 or 11 bankruptcies.

Valuation Analyses

Throughout the life cycle of a business, it is essential to know how much it is worth. For the financially distressed company, this becomes even more urgent. An appraisal is required both shortly before and after a business decides to go into bankruptcy. Business valuation professionals, or appraisers, are engaged to provide an objective estimate of what the business is worth, as well as provide other services that are crucial to management, shareholders, and creditors.

For example, the valuation analysis helps all parties understand the *fair market value* of the underlying tangible and intangible assets of the distressed business and assists them in making informed decisions. Appraisers also determine if reimbursement is necessary for any preferential transfers or fraudulent conveyance payments to vendors or other parties, and render such opinions during bankruptcy proceedings. The following section lays out the essentials of a business appraisal.

Tangible Assets

Physical assets that contribute to the economic benefits generated by business operations can include inventory, tools, equipment, office furniture, computers, and other electronics; manufacturing machinery and equipment; and processing equipment and vehicles. These tangible assets allow the business to deliver its products and services. Their value is examined and assessed based on the "premise of value;" i.e., going-concern, orderly liquidation, and forced liquidation.

The valuation of tangible assets is different for each business and industry. For example, in the professional services industry, a business will have minimal tangible assets, primarily comprising office furniture and computers; while companies in heavy manufacturing may have extensive and specialized equipment, designed for specific functions and purposes. Because in cases of default tangible assets can be recovered, lenders prefer them to secure debt. And although their value is typically first determined at loan origination, they will also be formally reappraised in bankruptcy.

Intangible Assets

Intangible assets are non-physical assets that grant rights and privileges to the business owner and include economic benefits.

Such assets are brand names, trademarks, patents, intellectual property, logos, customer lists, relationships and contracts, processes and procedures, and trained workforces, among others. For an intangible asset to have economic value, it must generate some measurable amount of economic benefit to its owner, and potentially enhance the value of other associated assets.

During a business valuation, the appraiser will work with management and ownership to understand and identify the intangible assets of a business. Experienced appraisers who are familiar with solvency and bankruptcy valuations will adeptly identify and appraise them. Often, the intangible assets retain the most value after a business ceases to operate.

Premise of Value

When performing valuation analyses for a distressed business or bankruptcy, the premise of value is determined by the context and conditions of the business. The four options include a *going-concern*, an *assemblage of assets*, an *orderly liquidation*, or a *forced liquidation*.

Valuation under a going-concern condition. In this scenario, the value of the business enterprise is determined by its continued use as a mass assemblage of income-producing assets and management. The going-concern enterprise includes the intangible elements that result from factors such as having a trained and well-managed workforce, an operational plant, and the necessary licenses, systems, and procedures in place.

Valuation as an assemblage of assets. The mass assemblage of assets not in current use in the production of income or as an ongoing business concern is measured as value-in-place. The American Society of Appraisers (ASA) Business Valuation Standards sometimes refer to this as the *net tangible* *asset value*—the value of a business enterprise's tangible assets (excluding excess assets and non-operating assets) minus the value of its liabilities.

Valuation as an orderly disposition. Value-in-exchange is determined on a piecemeal basis—apart from a mass assemblage of assets—as part of an orderly liquidation. The valuation is based on the net amount a business would realize upon termination when the assets are sold in an orderly manner over a reasonable period to maximize proceeds.

Valuation as a forced liquidation. Value in exchange is determined on a piecemeal basis—not part of a mass assemblage of assets. The valuation assumes that a business will sell its assets individually and quickly and experience less-than-normal market exposure. A chapter 7 bankruptcy liquidation and auction is one example of forced liquidation.

To value a business and its various assets, one must know what interests and assets must be evaluated and the assumptions that dictate the context of the appraisal.

Standard of Value

When performing a valuation analysis, a standard of value" should be used. The most commonly applied standards of value are *fair market value* and *fair value.*

The ASA Business Valuation Standards and the Uniform Standards of Professional Appraisal Practice (USPAP) define fair market value as "the price, expressed in terms of cash equivalents, at which property would change hands between a willing and able buyer and a hypothetical seller acting at arm's length in an open and unrestricted market, when neither is under compulsion to buy or sell and when both have reasonable knowledge of the relevant facts."

The Financial Accounting Standards Board (FASB) in Accounting Standards Codification (ASC) 820 defines fair value as "the price that would be received to sell an asset or paid to transfer a liability in an orderly transaction between market participants at the measurement date."

Typically, financial reporting uses the fair value standard, while solvency and bankruptcy valuations use the fair market value standard. However, the intended uses and users of each analysis will dictate the standard of value that is appropriate for the assignment.

Valuation Approaches

In general, there are three approaches for valuing business entities: (1) income approach, (2) market approach, and (3) asset-based approach. Valuation professionals use one to three of these approaches in each engagement, depending on the characteristics of the subject business.

Income approach. The income approach considers earnings or cash flow that assumes an investor could invest in an alternative asset with similar investment characteristics. The computations under the income approach determine whether the value of an asset is equal to the present value of anticipated future benefits. This approach is often seen in the form of capitalization of a selected income base or discounted future earnings or cash flow stream over a projection period.

Market approach. The market approach is a direct method for establishing an asset's fair market value. Under the market approach, the appraiser attempts to locate assets that have been sold to make comparisons of value. Also, in valuing the asset by the income or market approach, consideration is given to the quality and condition of the asset. An asset that produces goods or provides services should be in reasonably good condition. Otherwise, its value may need to be reduced to account for necessary capital expenditures to place the asset in an appropriate productive state.

Asset approach. The cost or asset approach to valuation considers the economic principle of *substitution*. This principle asserts that an investor will pay no more for an investment than the cost to obtain, either by purchase or by construction, an investment of equal utility. A willing buyer for an asset will pay no more for the subject asset than the price of a property with comparable service.

An appraiser will determine the approaches and methods most applicable to the business and its assets. Ultimately, the appraiser will consider the reliability and accuracy of each technique and reconcile the approach to conclude a final value.

Solvency Analyses and Solvency Opinion

Solvency analyses determine whether a business has sufficient assets, cash flow, and liquidity to meet its obligations at any given time. If it does not, the company is deemed insolvent. Although pretty straightforward, when an insolvent business subsequently files for bankruptcy things become complicated, quickly. Two of the most common complications occur if a business makes a preferential or fraudulent transfer of monies before bankruptcy.

Preferential Transfer

Section 547 of the United States Bankruptcy Code states, in part, that a preferential transfer is a transfer to a creditor within 90 days of a bankruptcy, when the creditor receives more than it would have if the transferor were liquated under a chapter 7 bankruptcy and the transfer was made when the transferor was insolvent or rendered insolvent as a result of the transfer. The 90-day period extends to one year for "insiders."

For example, if an insolvent business makes payments to vendors or other parties prior to filing for bankruptcy, such payments may be deemed preferential—debts paid to a particular creditor, taking preference over other creditors. If the business is found to have engaged in a preferential transfer, the "preferred" party that received payment is liable to pay it back to the company, or to other creditors affected by the debtor's bankruptcy.

Fraudulent Transfer

A fraudulent transfer, or fraudulent conveyance, may be either an actual fraudulent transfer, that is a transfer of an asset of the transferor with the actual intent to hinder, delay, or defraud a creditor. The transfer may also be a constructive fraudulent transfer, which is a transfer for less than reasonably equivalent value made at a time when the transferor

- was insolvent on the date of the transfer or such obligation incurred or became insolvent as a result;

- was engaged in business or a transaction, or was about to engage in business or a transaction, for which any property remaining with the transferor was an unreasonably small capital;

- was intended to incur, or believed that the transferor would incur, debts that would be beyond the transferor's ability to pay as such debts matured; or

- was made to or for the benefit of an insider, or incurred such obligation to or for the benefit of an insider, under an employment contract and not in the ordinary course of business.

Preferential transfers made within 90 days to one year before filing a petition may be subject to repayment. Fraudulent transfers made up to *two years* prior to the filing of a petition may be subject to repayment. In some cases, state laws allow for more extended periods of up to seven years before the transfer.

In a lawsuit for recovery of a preferential or fraudulent conveyance, the bankruptcy court will require a solvency analysis and opinion. Bankruptcy case law provides three tests of solvency which a business must pass:

1. **Balance Sheet Test.** The balance sheet test determines whether a company's asset value was greater than its total liabilities before and after the transaction in question.

2. **Adequate Capital Test.** The adequate capital test ascertains whether a company is likely to survive after the transaction in question, assuming reasonable business fluctuations in the future. To perform this test, the business appraiser conducts various stress tests to assess a business's capital and cash flow in future years.

3. **Cash Flow Test.** The cash flow test calculates whether a company incurred debts that were beyond its ability to pay as the debts matured. For this test, the business appraiser analyzes management's projections and cash flow and determines the likelihood of the business's ability to cover future debt payments.

In most cases, appraisers will perform the above solvency analyses and render a solvency opinion during bankruptcy proceedings to determine if there are reimbursable preferential transfer or fraudulent conveyance payments to vendors or other parties.

To put the above into context, consider the hypothetical case of Distressed Corp.

Valuation of Distressed Corp–A Case Study

Distressed Corp (DC) supplies rubber and plastic components, such as covers, seals, gaskets, tubes, housings, connectors, clips, and fasteners, to the automotive manufacturing industry. The company experienced steady growth since inception, due to its quality processes, talented staff, and relationships with key customers who design and develop engines, power transmission systems, and pumps to original equipment manufacturers' specifications.

After ten years in business, DC management was very confident that their most profitable customers had become dependent on DC's components and presented a low risk for defection. Even in the worst-case scenario, management believed that they could replace important customers quickly.

In 2013 DC obtained a $3 million loan to help fund its growth, payable over the next 10 years at a 5 percent annual interest rate. A year later (as shown in exhibit 1), company revenues increased from $32 million to $36 million. But in the two following years, DC's largest customer experienced a significant decrease in sales volumes, causing DC's revenues to drop $6 million in 2015 and another $4 million in 2016. During the same period, the direct cost of DC's materials and assembly operations increased from 75.1 percent of total revenues to 79.3 percent, causing the gross profit margin to decrease by 20.7 percent.

Compounding the situation, and counter to their expectations, DC was unable to secure a new customer to offset the declining revenues from its top customer. So the company set out to reduce costs, implement new technologies, and execute a plan to restructure and retool its operations. Indeed, upgraded technologies allowed DC to bid on new contracts, and management deployed aggressive marketing tactics to feature its new capabilities and obtain new customers to return the company to profitability. But, as exhibit 2 shows, its largest customer delayed invoice payments, and DC's 2015 cash balance decreased while its accounts receivable increased. In turn, DC began to delay payments to its vendors, causing 2015's accounts payable to increase by approximately $1 million from 2014 levels.

Accounts receivable and accounts payable slightly decreased in 2016 due to loss mitigation efforts by DC's management, but at the end of 2016, the total long-term debt held by DC was approximately $2 million (notes payable and current portion of notes payable).

Given the dramatic changes over the past few years, DC's creditors became concerned that the company could not fulfill the remainder of its debt obligations. Creditors then hired an outside business valuation firm to assess DC's financial position and determine its fair market value.

Exhibit 3 shows a cursory summary of the ratio analyses performed, which reflect DC's dire financial, liquidity, and profitability picture at the end of 2016. From 2013 to 2016, the company's current ratio and net working capital ratio decreased from 1.91 to 1.29, and 1.83 to 1.50, respectively. These ratios measured short-term liquidity; for example, whether assets could be converted into cash in less than one year in order to pay for liabilities that were due within the year.

Also, DC's interest coverage ratio (the measure of a company's ability to pay annual interest expenses) and debt coverage ratio (the measure of a company's ability to make annual interest *and* principal payments) were negative in 2016. These negative ratios indicated the company's inability to pay its annual debt service payments through profits earned that year. In other words, the company was technically insolvent.

Creditor Considerations

Despite the dire state of the company, DC management firmly believed that its newly devised turnaround plan would return the business to profitability. (Exhibit 4 presents management's projected income statement showing stabilized operations and reduced costs in 2017, breakeven operations in 2018, and significant profitability in 2019.)

After reviewing the company's anticipated financial position, its creditors had some options. One option was to restructure debt terms and allow DC to continue operations under a lower monthly and annual debt payment burden. In this scenario, an analysis of the business's post-restructuring solvency—the future financial position of the company—was crucial for lenders to understand. Although creditors may have been confident in management's post-restructuring cash flow projections, an independent appraiser was necessary to examine management's estimates and projections and opine on their reasonableness, as well as the company's future solvency, cash flow expectations, sales volume assumptions, cost reductions, and ability to retain valuable staff.

In DC's case, the total interest and principal payments in 2016 were approximately $345,000. Restructuring this debt to reduce annual payments could have helped DC reach a breakeven point sooner, and increase the prospects of full debt repayment in future years.

Debt-to-Equity Swap

Another option available to DC's creditors is a debt-to-equity swap, an exchange of outstanding debt for equity in a company. The financial feasibility of a debt-to-equity swap required a valuation of a 100-percent equity interest and a minority equity interest of less than 50 percent. The appraiser's role in a debt-to-equity swap process is also crucial, as the appraised value affects the ownership percentage that a creditor may assume in exchange for debt.

In evaluating a debt-to-equity swap, the appraiser must determine the fair market value of the business based upon the appropriate premise of value, the standard of value, and scope of the assignment, using the three valuation approaches discussed above. The appraiser also evaluates the fair market value of the minority interest, which includes discounts for lack of control and lack of marketability to account for a minority's limitations on control and illiquidity of shares.

In DC's case, let's assume the appraiser found that management's projections were reasonable. But, taking into account any risks associated with meeting those projections, the appraiser concluded that $3.5 million was the fair market value of a 100-percent equity interest in DC. (Under the most optimistic scenario, DC could have been worth up to $7 million.) With a total outstanding debt of $2 million in 2016, a partial debt-for-equity swap could have provided an opportunity for creditors to obtain ownership in the firm and benefit in its potential growth in value in the future.

Perhaps more importantly, the value of DC's tangible assets (exhibit 2) was relatively small compared to its outstanding debt, and would thus have yielded an insignificant return on a potential bankruptcy filing. Therefore, in this case, creditors felt confident to move forward with a swap.

Looking more closely at how this might work, let's say that the creditors decided on a 33.33-percent equity interest in the company in exchange for $800,000 of debt, approximately 40 percent of what was owed. Although the fair market value of 100-percent equity interest was $3.5 million, in the debt-to-equity swap a one-third equity interest in the company was valued at $800,000, not $1,166,667 ($3.5 million x 33.33% = $1,166,667).

This value reflects the total combined discounts for lack of control, lack of marketability, and illiquidity applicable to a minority interest in a closely held business. Such minority discounts can range widely from 10 percent to 50 percent, depending on the facts and circumstances associated with the subject interest and business. But in DC's case, the appraiser applied a *31-percent discount* to the pro rata value to conclude on the $800,000 swap value ($1,166,667 x 31% combined discount = $800,000). Under this proposed debt-to-equity swap, the creditors would have owned a one-third interest in DC and still have held a $1.2 million promissory note.

At the time of the swap, the value of the one-third interest was equal to the amount of debt exchanged. However, per the appraiser's estimates, if the business, under the most optimistic scenario, could have achieved its turnaround goals, the value of DC and the creditors' one-third equity interest could have potentially doubled. Creditors' ability to benefit in the company's future value is one reason a debt-to-equity swap may be a viable option for distressed businesses and their creditors.

Regardless which option a creditor may choose, an analysis of the company's cash flow, solvency picture, and fair market value provide critical financial information to the creditors and allow them to make educated and informed decisions.

Solvency Analysis

As mentioned earlier, three tests must be met for business solvency: the balance sheet test, adequate capital test, and cash flow test. Using the facts established in the fictional DC example, the following presents the application.

Balance sheet test. The balance sheet test assesses a company's asset value relative to its liabilities. To conduct this test, the business appraiser determines the total fair market value of the company's assets and subtracts the interest-bearing debt to calculate the net asset value of the company.

The balance sheet for DC (exhibit 2) shows that as of December 31, 2016, the book value of the company's total assets was roughly $6.38 million. The book value of its total liabilities was about $6.40 million. These facts suggest that under a forced sale or liquidation setting, the value of the company's assets would likely not exceed its liabilities. However, as mentioned earlier, an independent appraisal determined that DC's fair market value of equity (assets minus liabilities) under a going-concern premise was $3.5 million. Because the appraiser determined that DC's value based on ongoing operations after subtracting debt was positive, it met the balance sheet test.

Adequate capital test. The adequate capital test is commonly referred to as "stress testing," and determines a company's likelihood of future survival, assuming reasonable business fluctuations. To perform this test, the appraiser considers future cash flow, asset values and volatility, expected asset growth, debt repayment timing, amount of debt, loan covenants, the company's borrowing base, and sensitivity to the various assumptions made on management's projected financial statements.

For DC, the appraiser concluded on a $3.5 million going-concern value for the business, based on projections of future positive cash flow as shown in exhibit 4. In a solvency analysis, the appraiser also performs scenario tests that consider various growth rates for revenues and expenses, as well as different assumptions for the timing of debt repayments. This stress test would show the level at which DC could be likely to maintain solvent operations in future years.

In these fictional projections, the company would likely pass. However, there may be certain scenarios under which DC would not pass the test, necessitating further scrutiny and consideration by creditors.

Cash flow test. The cash flow test determines whether a company incurs debts that are beyond its ability to pay as the debts mature. To complete this test, the business appraiser analyzes the cash flow projections prepared by management. As summarized in exhibit 4, DC expected to stabilize operations over the next two years and return to profitability in year three. Similar to the adequate capital test analysis, the appraiser conducts various stress tests. In particular, the appraiser must examine the projection's key assumptions and opine on the business's ability to meet its future cash flow projections, assuming various debt repayment schedules.

A financial analysis of DC, based on its historical performance, suggested liquidity concerns. As shown in exhibit 3, in the past two years, DC's liquidity, profitability, and debt coverage ratios significantly decreased. If historical trends were to continue, DC would not cover its debt payments and continue to operate. But to the extent that management's turnaround plan works and debt holders are confident that its projected levels of profitability are feasible, it would be possible to realize positive liquidity and profitability.

These analyses are crucial for creditors because their primary focus is assessing whether a company can meet its debt repayment obligations. Based on this analysis, it is likely that DC would have passed this third test.

In summary, it appears that DC could have passed the three tests and have been deemed solvent by an appraiser. Still, alternate scenarios exist. Given this outcome, creditors have to decide on what option—debt restructuring, debt-to-equity swap, or no change at all—is best for both the business and the creditors, moving forward.

Conclusion

A challenged or distressed financial state has various causes. But the prospect of bankruptcy increases when a business encounters one of the Three Deadly Ls: loss of customers, lawsuit, or loading up on debt. Management's ability to recognize a potential threat to the business's cash flow and assets and implement a plan to withstand a financial blow can be the difference between a bad quarter and a full failure of the firm.

Whether a business is experiencing a temporary event, approaching bankruptcy, or currently engaged in bankruptcy court proceedings, it is necessary to perform valuation and solvency analyses. Both owners and creditors are obligated to assess the company's financial condition and determine what to expect going forward. Understanding how appraisers value a company's assets and how creditors evaluate a company's prospects is essential for business owners in financial distress. Engaging a qualified business valuation firm is crucial.

— ◇ —

Nevin Sanli is president and founder of Sanli Pastore & Hill, Inc. **Henry Kaskov** is managing director of the firm's Chicago office. SP&H is a financial consulting firm that specializes in business valuations, forensic accounting, fairness and solvency opinions, forensic finance and economics, expert testimony, brand and intellectual property valuations, and strategic consulting services for businesses, families, and individuals. In aggregate, SP&H's senior professionals have over 110 years of experience. The firm is headquartered in Los Angeles and has regional offices in Sacramento, San Diego, and Chicago. Contact Nevin Sanli at nsanli@sphvalue.com and Henry Kaskov at hkaskov@sphvalue.com.

EXHIBIT 1

Distressed Corp.

Historical Income Statements

	2013		2014		2015		2016	
Total Revenues	$32,405,467	100.0%	$36,506,159	100.0%	$30,025,065	100.0%	$25,804,353	100.0%
Cost of Sales	$24,336,506	75.1%	$28,000,224	76.7%	$23,419,551	78.0%	$20,462,852	79.3%
Gross Profit	$8,068,961	24.9%	$8,505,935	23.3%	$6,605,514	22.0%	$5,341,501	20.7%
Operating Expenses								
Operations	$5,985,164	18.5%	$6,100,138	16.7%	$5,653,649	18.8%	$5,089,153	19.7%
Personnel	1,164,913	3.6%	1,269,507	3.5%	1,220,490	4.1%	980,134	3.8%
Advertising and Marketing	78,652	0.2%	85,679	0.2%	82,642	0.3%	52,469	0.2%
General and Administrative	175,136	0.5%	276,149	0.8%	252,349	0.8%	198,435	0.8%
Total Operating Expenses	$7,403,865	22.8%	$7,731,473	21.2%	$7,209,130	24.0%	$6,320,191	24.5%
EBITDA	$665,096	2.1%	$774,462	2.1%	($603,616)	-2.0%	($978,690)	-3.8%
Depreciation and Amortization	$42,779	0.1%	$42,803	0.1%	$42,991	0.1%	$42,155	0.2%
EBIT	$622,317	1.9%	$731,659	2.0%	($646,607)	-2.2%	($1,020,845)	-4.0%
Interest Expense	$133,019	0.4%	$122,444	0.3%	$111,339	0.4%	$99,680	0.4%
Pre-Tax Income / (Loss)	**$489,298**	1.5%	**$609,215**	1.7%	**($757,946)**	-2.5%	**($1,120,525)**	-4.3%

EXHIBIT 2
Distressed Corp.
Historical Balance Sheet

	2013		2014		2015		2016	
Assets								
Current Assets								
Cash and Cash Equivalents	$689,298	9.5%	$1,266,724	15.6%	$508,778	6.2%	($611,747)	-9.6%
Accounts Receivable	1,878,226	25.9%	2,094,698	25.7%	2,429,601	29.7%	2,251,833	35.3%
Inventory	3,458,466	47.8%	3,509,273	43.1%	4,082,141	49.9%	3,718,962	58.3%
Prepaid Expenses	750,075	10.4%	785,461	9.6%	723,164	8.8%	630,013	9.9%
Total Current Assets	$6,776,065	93.6%	$7,656,156	94.0%	$7,743,683	94.6%	$5,989,061	93.8%
Fixed, Net								
Equipment & Software	$427,511	5.9%	$384,708	4.7%	$341,717	4.2%	$299,562	4.7%
Other Fixed Asset	0	0.0%	62,181	0.8%	60,006	0.7%	57,831	0.9%
Total Fixed, Net	$427,511	5.9%	$446,889	5.5%	$401,723	4.9%	$357,393	5.6%
Other Assets								
Other Assets, Net	$37,192	0.5%	$38,308	0.5%	$36,301	0.4%	$36,085	0.6%
Total Other Assets	$37,192	0.5%	$38,308	0.5%	$36,301	0.4%	$36,085	0.6%
Total Assets	**$7,240,768**	100.0%	**$8,141,352**	100.0%	**$8,181,707**	100.0%	**$6,382,539**	100.0%

EXHIBIT 2 (Continued)
Distressed Corp.
Historical Balance Sheet

Liabilities and Equity							
Current Liabilities							
Accounts Payable	$3,297,145	45.5%	$3,786,512	46.5%	$4,789,019	58.5%	$4,349,603	68.1%
Accrued Expenses	34,100	0.5%	47,615	0.6%	65,497	0.8%	59,462	0.9%
Current Portion of Note Payable	211,513	2.9%	222,088	2.7%	233,193	2.9%	244,852	3.8%
Total Current Liabilities	$3,542,758	48.9%	$4,056,215	49.8%	$5,087,709	62.2%	$4,653,917	72.9%
Long-Term Liabilities							
Note Payable	$2,448,872	33.8%	$2,226,784	27.4%	$1,993,591	24.4%	$1,748,739	27.4%
Total Long-Term Liabilities	$2,448,872	33.8%	$2,226,784	27.4%	$1,993,591	24.4%	$1,748,739	27.4%
Total Liabilities	$5,991,631	82.7%	$6,282,999	77.2%	$7,081,300	86.6%	$6,402,656	100.3%
Stockholders' Equity							
Retained Earnings (Losses)	$759,840	10.5%	$1,249,138	15.3%	$1,858,353	22.7%	$1,100,407	17.2%
Net Profit	$489,298	6.8%	$609,215	7.5%	($757,946)	-9.3%	($1,120,525)	-17.6%
Total Stockholders' Equity	$1,249,138	17.3%	$1,858,353	22.8%	$1,100,407	13.4%	($20,118)	-0.3%
Total Liabilities and Stockholders' Equity	$7,240,768	100.0%	$8,141,352	100.0%	$8,181,707	100.0%	$6,382,538	100.0%

EXHIBIT 3

Distressed Corp.
Ratio Analysis

	2013	2014	2015	2016
Liquidity				
Current Ratio				
Current Assets / Current Liabilities	1.91	1.89	1.52	1.29
% Change		*−1.3%*	*−19.4%*	*−15.4%*
Net Working Capital Ratio				
Cash-Free Current Assets / Debt-Free Current Liabilities	1.83	1.67	1.49	1.50
% Change		*−8.8%*	*−10.6%*	*0.5%*
Interest Coverage Ratio				
EBIT / Interest Expense	4.68	5.98	−5.81	−10.24
Debt Coverage Ratio				
EBITDA / (Debt Interest & Principal Payment)	1.93	2.25	−1.75	−2.84
Shareholder Equity Ratio				
Total Stockholders' Equity / Total Assets	0.17	0.23	0.13	−0.00
Profitability				
EBIT (Schedule 1)	$622,317	$731,659	($646,607)	($1,020,845)
EBIT Margin	*1.9%*	*2.0%*	*−2.2%*	*−4.0%*
EBITDA (Schedule 1)	$665,096	$774,462	($603,616)	($978,690)
EBITDA Margin	*2.1%*	*2.1%*	*−2.0%*	*−3.8%*
Return on Assets (ROA)	*6.8%*	*7.5%*	*−9.3%*	*−17.6%*
Net Income / Total Assets				
Return on Equity (ROE)	*39.2%*	*32.8%*	*−68.9%*	*NM*
Net Income / Total Equity				

EXHIBIT 4

Distressed Corp.
Projected Income Statements

	2017		2018		2019	
Total Revenues	$27,000,000	100.0%	$28,500,000	100.0%	$31,546,191	100.0%
Cost of Sales	$21,006,000	77.8%	$21,916,500	76.9%	$23,785,828	75.4%
Gross Profit	$5,994,000	22.2%	$6,583,500	23.1%	$7,760,363	24.6%
Operating Expenses						
Operations	$4,914,000	18.2%	$5,105,000	17.9%	$5,331,306	16.9%
Personnel	999,000	3.7%	1,054,500	3.7%	1,135,663	3.6%
Advertising and Marketing	57,857	0.2%	65,791	0.2%	70,164	0.2%
General and Administrative	204,134	0.8%	235,619	0.8%	257,164	0.8%
Total Operating Expenses	$6,174,991	22.9%	$6,460,910	22.7%	$6,794,297	21.5%
EBITDA	($180,991)	−0.7%	$122,590	0.4%	$966,066	3.1%
Depreciation and Amortization	$42,155	0.2%	$42,155	0.1%	$42,155	0.1%
EBIT	($223,146)	−0.8%	$80,435	0.3%	$923,911	2.9%
Interest Expense	$87,437	0.3%	$74,582	0.3%	$61,085	0.2%
Pre-Tax Income / (Loss)	($310,583)	−1.2%	$5,853	0.0%	$862,826	2.7%

8

Sale Transactions

BY JEFFREY A. KRIEGER

W hen a business can no longer meet its immediate fiscal responsibilities, selling some or all of its enterprise is likely. The troubled company may decide to sell limited assets to repay an essential creditor, to sell the entire business in bankruptcy as a going concern, or to liquidate in a piecemeal fashion at auction. Whether through federal bankruptcy court proceedings, a state-law governed assignment for the benefit of creditors, or an informal resolution with the company's creditors, the financially distressed company will consider a sale transaction as one of its potential exit strategies.

Sale transactions can be a critical tool for the distressed business. Although parts of the sale process are the same as a typical corporate asset sale by a financially healthy seller, it is vital for a company in financial distress to understand the differences. This chapter will focus principally on the particular issues that arise in the sale of assets in chapter 11 bankruptcy.

— ◇ —

When to Sell Assets

A company is considered in financial distress when it is insolvent, or nearing insolvency. A company in debt to its creditors is the "debtor." A debtor company, represented by its management, controlling shareholders, or members, is obligated under U.S. bankruptcy law to maximize value for the best outcome for its stakeholders. A company's stakeholders consist of equity holders, secured and unsecured creditors, and employees.

Often, a debtor that is unable to continue as an operating company without losing money may still own valuable assets. Or, although a debtor may be unable to fund critical operations, such as payroll, a third party with liquidity might use the company's assets and generate profit.

If a debtor is unable to solve its financial problem through a restructuring, a loan, or equity infusion, it should look to maximize value for its stakeholders through a sale of assets. By selling the assets, a debtor can create a recovery for creditors, who might otherwise receive very little or nothing at all. And, in the best scenario, the asset purchaser will enhance its existing business with those newly acquired assets and employ the debtor's former employees, who would otherwise lose their jobs.

Asset Sales under Chapter 11

In bankruptcy, section 363 of the U.S. Bankruptcy Code governs asset sales. Commonly referred to as "363 sales," the process allows a debtor in chapter 11 or a trustee in chapter 7 to sell assets outside the ordinary course of business after obtaining bankruptcy court approval.

A 363 sale can maximize the value realized in a sale of assets because it provides for the seller's right to sell "free and clear" of any claims against, or interest in, such property. A buyer will often pay more for assets that are unencumbered by the seller's liabilities, as it allows the buyer to move forward and exploit its purchase without the seller company's debt burden.

Over the past several decades, asset sales through bankruptcy have become more common than other chapter 11 exit strategies. Part of the reason for this is that bankruptcy judges had previously limited a debtor's ability to sell assets outside of a confirmed plan of reorganization. Selling assets through a plan of reorganization is a much longer and more expensive process. However, courts now recognize that it is more practical and less costly to permit stand-alone bankruptcy sales and allow them with much higher frequency. Today, distressed-asset purchasers are primarily hedge funds and other opportunistic financial parties who are skilled in the bankruptcy sale process. These parties, typically, are not willing to endure the delay and cost of a sale through a plan of reorganization.

Today, nearly every type of asset that a company might own can be sold through a section 363 sale, from real property to physical inventory and from intellectual property to manufacturing equipment and accounts receivable.

The 363 Process

A 363 sale usually involves a two-step judicial process whereby the seller asks the court (1) to *approve how the sale proceeds* and (2) to *approve the sale of assets* to the buyer.

In most instances, the debtor first enters into a contract of sale with a buyer, known as the "stalking horse" in bankruptcy parlance. The term stems from the 16th-century practice in which hunters would stalk their prey by hiding behind a horse, and it has evolved to signify the party who is selected by the debtor as the initial bidder for its assets. The stalking-horse bid plays an important role in the process, as it is meant to provoke others bidders while eliminating low bids. From the debtor's point of view, the stalking horse provides a level of certainty, a base price at which the assets will be sold, and creates an aura that there is a market for the assets. From the buyer's perspective, certain protections for the stalking horse mitigate some of the risks associated with being a purchaser in a bankruptcy case. At the bankruptcy auction, the stalking horse may end up being the ultimate buyer, or the buyer could be another party that overbids the stalking horse buyer.

Sometimes a debtor is unable to locate a willing stalking-horse buyer or negotiate a sale agreement with the stalking horse. In this case, the debtor may ask the bankruptcy court to allow a straight auction, with no stalking horse. Although straight auctions only occur in a minority of chapter 11 cases—because the debtor is not sure that it will receive at least a minimum sale price—there is nothing in the bankruptcy code that prohibits this type of sale.

Identifying Assets for Sale

The most typical chapter 11 sale involves substantially all of the debtor's assets in the bankruptcy estate. The phrase "substantially all" is used in sale contracts because often the debtor will not include negligible assets or expressly exclude valuable assets. In the latter circumstance, the sale contract must identify excluded assets.

In some instances, a sale contract might describe the specific acquired assets. However, when a sale contract for substantially all assets also defines acquired assets and excluded assets, it can cause ambiguity and disagreement between parties and other prospective buyers over what is for sale. Therefore, sellers and buyers must carefully consider definitions to avoid future disputes.

Differences Between a Healthy Sale Transaction and a 363 Sale

Both the financially sound and distressed business will approach the business sale similarly: they will market their assets to find a buyer. However, the 363 sale proceeds differently. A crucial difference is that the sale agreement between a distressed business and a buyer is conditional. The sale itself is subject to bankruptcy court approval for final enforcement, and several other steps are typically necessary before closing the sale.

For example, although not required by any bankruptcy statute or rule, 363 sales are nearly always structured as "subject to overbid." In other words, because the court's job is to ensure that the debtor obtains maximum value for assets sold, if it believes that other interested buyers might overbid the original purchase price agreement and prevail, it will not approve the debtor's initial sale agreement. Accordingly, a 363 asset sale agreement, at least for an ongoing business, uniformly will include language and a process for overbidding. Depending on the facts and circumstances of the case, typically when only a single unique asset is for sale and there is likely no broad market for the asset, the overbid is unnecessary. The seller will, however, have to satisfy the court that overbidding is not necessary.

Limited Seller Representations and Warranties

A solvent seller in a typical sale transaction will ordinarily provide multiple representations and warranties that protect the buyer. If the seller breaches a representation or warranty, the buyer has recourse against the seller, even if, in some cases, the contract legally limits it.

In a 363 sale, however, not only is the scope of the representations typically far more limited than in a non-bankruptcy sale, but the bankruptcy estate is likely financially unable to compensate the buyer for any significant damages in the event of a breach. Thus, as a practical matter, whether stated or not, generally the 363 sale is considered "as is, where is." A buyer should accordingly conduct prudent due diligence into the assets of a seller debtor and adjust its purchase price accordingly.

Stalking Horse

Another difference between a solvent company's sale agreement and the 363 sale contract is that in the latter the stalking horse, if there is one, is usually able to negotiate individual protections to support its early bid and to reimburse its expenses if it is not the successful bidder. Because the stalking horse will make a significant up-front investment of time and money on due diligence to determine an appropriate purchase price and negotiate the form of sale agreement—often with the assistance of expensive professionals—these protections will compensate for the very genuine possibility that it might not become the winning bidder. Unlike the sale of a solvent company, the stalking-horse bidder will rarely get the benefit of a "lock up" or exclusivity, wherein for a period of time after the signing of the purchase agreement, the debtor company is "locked up" and may only deal exclusively with the stalking-horse buyer. To the contrary, as noted above, almost uniformly, a 363 sale is expressly subject to overbidding.

Commonly, the stalking horse's willingness to step forward and establish a purchase-price floor makes other bidders more comfortable and encourages bidding. Because this can enhance the value of the assets for the benefit of the bankruptcy estate, leading to a more robust auction and a higher sale price, courts recognize that certain protections are a fair *quid pro quo* for the stalking horse. Furthermore, having a stalking-horse bidder streamlines the auction process, as other interested buyers will be able to use, or often be required to use, the form of the agreement negotiated by the stalking horse when they submit initial overbids. A standard form allows the seller to compare, more efficiently, apples to apples in the bidding process.

Typical stalking-horse protections include a breakup fee, expense reimbursement, a minimum initial overbid amount, a minimum overbid increment, and various financial restrictions on who may become a qualified bidder" Other negotiated protections might require that any overbid includes the same complete package of assets and no piecemeal bids. From a policy standpoint, overbid protections encourage stalking horses, which can benefit bankruptcy estates. However, the same protections, if taken too far, can reduce competition at the auction and subsequently minimize asset value. In deciding which protections to approve, the bankruptcy court must balance competing concerns.

Breakup up fees. A breakup fee is paid by the seller to the stalking horse (usually directly from sale proceeds) if it is not the ultimate winning bidder. The breakup fee is designed to compensate the stalking horse for being the first to agree to buy the assets and "priming the pump" for other bidders. The debtor and stalking horse negotiate this fee at the time of the sale agreement. Statutory law does not define a reasonable breakup fee; however, case law has established that 3 percent of the contract purchase price as a customary maximum.

Expense reimbursement. Similar to a breakup fee, the expense reimbursement is calculated based upon out-of-pocket expenses incurred by the stalking horse in connection with due diligence and sale agreement negotiations. The stalking horse receives this fee only if it is not the winning bidder. In some cases, the expense reimbursement is subsumed within the breakup fee and used as a further justification for the amount of the breakup fee.

To illustrate how this works, let's look at the THQ bankruptcy in Delaware, in which a private equity firm stalking horse offered to acquire "substantially all" of the game developer's assets. The offer was sufficient to pay both secured and administrative priority claims, but a very spirited, two-day auction ensued. Multiple parties purchased various assets. Upon its conclusion, the stalking horse was no longer the buyer and walked away with a combined breakup fee and expense reimbursement of $1.5 million.

Minimum initial overbid increments and minimum overbid amounts. A stalking horse will seek to impose as large a minimum initial overbid increment as possible, hoping to reduce competition for the assets. However, an excessive initial overbid amount can have a negative impact on bidding. The seller and the bankruptcy court will be wary of this happening, as it is their job to ensure a healthy return on assets to satisfy creditors. Still, the minimum initial overbid increment needs to be at least as large as, and slightly more than, the amount of the breakup fee.

Concerning the size of each increment for subsequent overbidding, stalking horses can have differing views. The size of these increments cuts both ways, because after the initial overbid increment the stalking horse is allowed to re-enter the bidding if it chooses and may become an overbidder itself. If the stalking horse is willing to pay more than what was initially offered and agreed to in the sale agreement, as is usually the case, the stalking horse may not want the overbid increments to be too large. Ultimately, the dollar amount will depend upon the particular dynamics of the situation, especially the opening purchase price. For example, if the sale is in the millions of dollars, a minimum overbid amount of at least $100,000 probably makes sense for all participants.

The qualified bidder. Another way the stalking horse seeks to tilt the playing field in its favor is to restrict the ability of third parties to become qualified bidders. Nearly all stalking-horse sale agreements define bidder qualifications and provide that only qualified bidders are eligible to participate in the auction.

Qualified bidder requirements usually include a substantial cash deposit to demonstrate to the seller's satisfaction the bidder's financial ability to close the transaction. An executed agreement in the same form used by the stalking horse is also often required, redlined to show any changes. The greater the number of changes, the greater the concern on the buyer's part that the seller may not consider the offer in the same favorable light as the stalking horse agreement. In most cases, the bidder must also provide proof that its representative, who will appear at the auction, has the legal authority to bind the bidder to the transaction.

Although generally the seller will prefer less stringent requirements than the stalking horse seeks to impose, it would not want standards so relaxed that a winning bidder might not close the transaction. Moreover, bankruptcy courts recognize the inherent unfairness to the stalking horse and all legitimate bidders based upon the artificial increase in price that could result if one bidder is allowed to participate and bid up the price even though it cannot close. Therefore, reasonable barriers to entry into the auction are nearly always approved by the bankruptcy court at the bid procedures hearing.

The bid procedure hearing. Most stalking-horse agreements state a certain time period for the debtor to file both a bid procedure motion and an asset sale motion. The bankruptcy court first holds a hearing on the bid procedures, at which it listens to arguments from interested parties about the pros and cons of the stalking-horse protections and makes a ruling on which ones are acceptable and which ones are rejected or must be modified. The court also establishes a date for the auction and for the hearing to approve the asset sale to the winning bidder. The timing of the auction and the sale hearing depends upon the financial exigencies.

Conditional Stalking-Horse Agreement

Consistent with section 363, the bankruptcy court must approve the stalking-horse agreement. Even if the debtor and a buyer agree to a sale of assets and enter into an agreement to sell, there is no such sale until the court approves it. This "subject to court approval" concept created an unusual problem in 2016 in the case of Hot Dog on a Stick.

A somewhat iconic fast-food restaurant, Hot Dog on a Stick (HDOS), ran into financial difficulties after more than 70 years in business. After filing chapter 11 and determining that a sale would be its most effective exit strategy, HDOS entered into a sale agreement with a stalking horse for $10 million cash and equity valued by HDOS at an additional $6 million. The sale agreement was subject to court approval and overbid, and required HDOS to file motions seeking approval of bid procedures and of the sale itself. The negotiated bid procedures included a $648,000 breakup fee.

Prior to HDOS' obtaining approval of the breakup fee, the court held a case status conference at which both the bankruptcy court and the creditors' committee expressed specific concerns about the pending sale agreement. The parties then attempted to negotiate a modified agreement but were unable to do so. For reasons that were in dispute among the parties, HDOS elected to enter into a new deal with another buyer and sought court approval of bid procedures with the new buyer. Over the objection of the first buyer, the bankruptcy court approved the second buyer as the stalking horse.

When the sale to the second buyer was approved, the first buyer made a claim for damages of $24 million against HDOS, based upon its expected profits under the agreement. As a fall-back position, it requested payment of the negotiated breakup fee of $648,000. The creditors' committee objected. The issue before the court was whether the first buyer had any rights under its agreement because the court had never approved it.

Although the case law on this issue is very sparse, it seems inconceivable that the court would award significant specula-tive damages. However, concerning the breakup fee, both par-ties had very reasonable arguments in their favor. On the one hand, there was no court approval, so perhaps no obligation at all. On the other hand, the debtor was obligated to seek court approval, which it failed to do. It is not surprising that the par-ties settled their dispute, with the bankruptcy estate's agreeing to pay $250,000.

This case demonstrates that despite the conditional nature of a stalking horse agreement, the debtor probably has an obli-gation to seek court approval of the sale.

Auction

After establishing bid procedures, if prospective bidders become qualified bidders, then the auction is held on the date set in the bid procedure order. If no qualified bidders emerge by the court's deadline, then the auction sale is canceled. After that, subject only to approval from the court at the sale hearing, the stalking horse will become the approved buyer of the assets.

If the auction proceeds, several variables set the stage.

When the scope of the assets for sale is rather small or uncomplicated, and depending on the practice in a particular jurisdiction, the judge might hold the auction in the bankruptcy courtroom and preside. Alternately, the judge may merely choose to observe, and the debtor's attorney will act as auctioneer.

When the volume of assets for sale is large or there are anticipated complications, such as issues or ground rules to resolve before the bidding can commence, auctions are conducted at the offices of the debtor's law firm or some other location, without the judge's presence. Again, the place of the auction may wholly be dependent on jurisdiction.

The early stages of the auction can alternate between general meetings of all parties in the main auction room and private meetings between the debtor's representatives and each qualified bidder. In large or complex cases, the debtor will retain an investment banker to advise or assist in marketing assets and to be involved in the auction process. Each qualified bidder is typically provided a conference room in which to caucus privately with its representatives. Likewise, private rooms are assigned to allow discussions among the investment bankers, counsel for the debtor, and their representatives.

A sort of shuttle diplomacy is undertaken to work out ground rules in an orderly manner. The debtor's representatives move from room to room to obtain clarifications of each party's opening bid and to perhaps negotiate issues and ensure that the qualified bidders are bidding on the same package of assets. Once all preliminary problems are worked out, the actual bidding commences.

The early portion of the auction can be quite fluid, and no two auctions are alike. Commonly, the debtor's investment bankers must sort out some difficult issues, such as how to conduct an auction when the stalking horse is seeking to acquire substantially all of the debtor's assets and others are interested only in very specific assets. As illustrated earlier, the THQ bankruptcy is a perfect example.

When THQ filed chapter 11, it entered into a stalking-horse agreement with Clearlake Capital LP to purchase "substantially all" of the debtor's assets, which consisted primarily of well-known video games and associated intellectual property rights. Clearlake's stalking-horse agreement provided that all overbids closely track the structure of Clearlake's bid, in effect precluding bidding on individual assets. But the creditors' committee objected. They argued that a piecemeal sale would result in more bidding and thus a better recovery for unsecured creditors. The court agreed with the creditors' committee and allowed bids on individual assets.

The court's ruling left THQ's investment bankers the unenviable task of determining how to run an auction in which some bidders wanted the entire business and others only specific assets. Due to the complexities of this scenario, parties worked well past midnight on auction day to sort out the procedure, and the actual bidding did not commence until the next day.

Once the bidding began, parties required multiple breaks and further caucusing and diplomacy before finally concluding late that afternoon, just minutes before the already rescheduled sale hearing was set to commence. Luckily, the auction site was just down the street from the courthouse, and all parties made it to the sale hearing in time.

At the hearing, the court approved the sales to multiple winning bidders, each of whom had acquired individual assets. None of the buyers was the original stalking horse.

Ultimately, the total net recovery for the bankruptcy estate and creditors was dramatically higher than the stalking-horse bid, thus justifying the position of the creditors' committee regarding the values and the process.

Approval of Sale

When bidding is complete and a winning bidder (or bidders, as in the THQ bankruptcy) has emerged from the auction, the court must still approve the sale.

First, the court will orally approve the sale of assets at the sale hearing. After that, the seller and the debtor will prepare or finalize a form of written sale order. The final order contains the court's findings and serves as notice to interested parties of the sale and auction's sufficiency. The written sale order will attest that the winning bidder acquired the assets in good faith; that the bid was highest and best offer; that the debtor had the power and authority to transfer the assets; and that the assets were free and clear of interests. The sale order also directs the debtor to transfer the assets to the winning bidder and prohibits the debtor's creditors from making claims against the winning bidder.

Strict prohibition against collusion among bidders. Section 363(n) of the U.S. Bankruptcy Code allows a debtor seller to "undo" a sale that is the result of collusion among bidders. This rule can initially cause some difficulty for bidders who are considering aligning with another party in a joint bid. Experienced bankruptcy counsel should be consulted to advise of the risks of entering into a joint bid.

The prohibition-against-collusion rule is designed to ensure that the value realized at auction is not suppressed by potential bidders choosing not to bid against each other, but instead to work together in a manner that affects the bidding. If a debtor believes that there has been any improper collaboration and that the value obtained has been improperly suppressed, it may file a motion with the court to unwind a sale. Collusion penalties are severe and include recovery of the difference in price, attorneys' fees, and punitive damages. Therefore, the statute accomplishes its objective and bidders rarely collude.

Closing and Final Order

Once the court enters the written sale order, the closing commences. This procedure establishes the date that assets transfer from owner to buyer. The sale agreement between the debtor and the winning bidder sets the closing date.

Usually, parties want to close the sale as soon as possible after the judge signs the written sale order. If there has been spirited bidding and, possibly, disagreement among the various parties, the statutory law allows parties to file a sale order appeal within 14 days. Without an appeal, after the 15th day, the sale order becomes final, that is no longer subject to appeal or review. But what if the parties want to close the sale before waiting for 15 days to avoid an appeal?

Stay pending appeal and good faith finding. A "stay pending appeal" is a court order that temporarily suspends court proceedings or the effect of a judgment. A party files a motion for a stay pending appeal when it wants to stop all proceedings in a case while waiting for an appellate court to hear its argument.

Buyers of assets in a bankruptcy case typically request a section 363(m) finding of good faith. If the sale order includes such a finding—a result reached by a judge based on the facts—then a reversal on appeal may not invalidate the sale unless the appellant also obtains a stay pending appeal. Because an appellant may have difficulty meeting the standard for a stay pending appeal, the 363(m) finding is important. Recently, however, courts have interpreted section 363(m) quite narrowly, eroding the protections provided by that statute. Nevertheless, it is still important for a buyer to request a 363(m) finding.

Exit Strategies

Over the past several years, the retail industry has been especially active in bankruptcy proceedings, liquidating assets through 363 sales. Examples include Gordmans stores, Gander Mountain, RadioShack, HHGregg, BCBG Max Azria, Michigan Sporting Goods Distributors, Eastern Outfitters, Wet Seal, Limited Stores, Payless, B&B Bachrach, Aeropostale, American Apparel, Sports Authority, Sports Chalet, Deb Shops, Delia's, Body Central, Toys "R" Us, and more. In most of these cases, the debtors used bankruptcies to conduct store closings or going-out-of-business type sales at multiple locations, among other things.

Debtors conducting going-out-of-business sales face some issues which include both contractual and statutory restrictions. For example, most commercial leases prohibit going-out-of-business sales. In addition, most states and local governments heavily regulate going-out-of-business sales, including restrictions regarding methods, timing, signage, and advertising. These laws also address consumer protection and health and safety concerns.

Although a going-out-of-business sale can occur outside of bankruptcy, it can be much easier to conduct one through bankruptcy. A bankruptcy court can enter orders that allow the seller to hold a sale notwithstanding such lease prohibitions and statutory regulations. Moreover, the U.S. Bankruptcy Code limits the damages that landlords can assert when a debtor closes a store. In recent years, financially sophisticated landlords have increasingly developed various protocols that allow for a reasonable amount of certainty and less litigation.

Beyond chapter 11 and the 363 asset sale, financially distressed or debtor companies have a few other available options to meet their obligations. In certain circumstances, an assignment for the benefit of creditors can be highly effective. See chapter 9 of this book for details on assignments for the benefit of creditors.

Distressed asset sales can also occur outside of formal insolvency proceedings, but may encounter contractual restrictions. For example, many business agreements and most leases contain anti-assignment clauses, prohibiting or restricting a party from assigning its rights under that agreement. These provisions are enforceable outside of bankruptcy, however, in a bankruptcy proceeding, subject only to a few exceptions, anti-assignment clauses are unenforceable. Therefore, a bankruptcy debtor can create value from a contract or lease by selling it to a third party, even when it is prohibited from doing so by the terms of the contract or lease.

An example of when an out-of-court strategy might be useful occurs when a company has equipment that is no longer being used but still has marketplace value. The company can sell those underutilized assets to pay down debt to a secured creditor or critical business partner. Retailers sometimes apply this strategy when underperforming stores are damaging well-performing stores. Without entering into an insolvency proceeding, the retailer might negotiate special arrangements with landlords to close underperforming stores and restructure by liquidating excess inventory to improve its financial profile.

In almost any financially distressed circumstance, the key is to use every tool at hand to achieve a desirable outcome and, importantly, to act fast. At the first sign of your business's being unable to meet its financial obligations, you should seek and heed a professional's advice.

— ◇ —

Jeffrey Krieger is a business lawyer specializing in bankruptcy-related matters, who represents secured creditors, unsecured creditors, landlords, chapter 11 debtors, trustees, and other parties in interest in federal bankruptcy and other insolvency proceedings. He also advises clients on minimizing financial risk when entering into a variety of types of agreements, including loan agreements, purchase and sale agreements, joint venture agreements, and settlement agreements. In addition to creating solutions for clients who have already entered into transactions with troubled companies, and representing them in proceedings before the U.S. Bankruptcy Court, Mr. Krieger also represents investors who are acquiring distressed assets both in- and -outside of bankruptcy proceedings. Contact him at <u>jkrieger@ greenbergglusker.com</u>.

9

General Assignments as an Effective Liquidation Device

By Joel B. Weinberg

A company facing extreme financial distress, such that continuing to operate the business is no longer viable, will typically choose from one of several options to liquidate assets and pay its creditors.

Among those options is "self-help," or a winding down of operations without a formal legal process. In a wind-down, company owners or officers, on their own, liquidate all assets of the company and then distribute the proceeds to its creditors. Although a wind-down avoids many costs and complexities associated with a legal proceeding, except in the simplest of cases, it is usually a less desirable option for several reasons.

Without a formal framework, creditors face no legal impediment to enforcing their claims. Therefore, a wind-down often fails in the face of collection efforts by creditors. Moreover, a wind-down requires that at least one officer remain to handle the wind down and who would be responsible for communicating with the company's creditors. Often, however, by the time they have reached this point after having exhausted all other alternatives, management of the business wants to move on and does not want to continue to be burdened by having to monitor and manage the wind-down. And critically, without the protections of a legal process, the company's board of directors will face exposure to third-party claims during the wind-down.

One legal alternative to a wind-down, which does employ a legal process, is a chapter 7 bankruptcy, discussed in greater detail in chapter 1 of this book. A chapter 7 bankruptcy is under federal law and sometimes may be the appropriate method for winding down a company.

Another option is a state-law general assignment for the benefit of creditors. The general assignment process provides a distressed enterprise a viable, efficient, and cost-effective pathway for liquidating its assets and distributing proceeds. A substantial benefit of an assignment is the potential for a sale of its assets as a "going concern," which can be used to maximize asset values. (A company's value as an ongoing entity is usually greater than its component pieces, because an ongoing operation can continue to earn a profit, while a liquidated company cannot.)

Unlike the uniform application of a federal bankruptcy throughout the country, the law of general assignments varies from state to state. Although a general assignment offers unique benefits and opportunities, it can also present pitfalls for the unwary. Two considerations typically govern the choice of a general assignment. First, sale transactions can be concluded more expeditiously than would be the case in either a bankruptcy or receivership. Second, less publicity surrounds the sale. This latter consideration is attractive to potential buyers who seek to avoid an erosion of the customer base and maintain going-concern value.

To illustrate, consider the case of a large regional auto part distributor that opted for a general assignment and had located a buyer, a prominent industry player. The auto part company had over 300 employees, operated more than 18 retail stores, and maintained several sizable retail warehouse distribution centers. The company's assets were encumbered by a blanket security interest in favor of its institutional lender, which was owed over $18 million. Under a general assignment, in less than a week and without prior notice or court intervention, the company achieved the following:

- they retained the assignee;

- negotiated the interim operating agreements to facilitate the smooth transition of operations for the next 180 days after assignment;

- negotiated a cash collateral agreement with the lender so that the assignment estate would have sufficient operating capital;

- assigned leases and key executory contracts to the buyer; and

- negotiated and concluded a definitive purchase agreement, allowing for the going-concern transition to a national third-party buyer.

The net result preserved and monetized the going-concern value, paid in the full the institutional secured lender and priority claim holders, and distributed significant dividends to unsecured creditors.

General Assignments under State Law

General assignments, while analogous to liquidation cases filed under chapter 7 of the bankruptcy code, follow state and not federal law. In its most straightforward sense, an assignment is a liquidation device available to an insolvent company as an alternative to formal bankruptcy proceedings. It is primarily a trust, whereby the debtor (assignor) assigns all of its assets to an assignee to act as a fiduciary for the benefit of the assignor's general unsecured creditors, who are the beneficiaries. The assignee liquidates the assignor's property and distributes the proceeds to creditors, according to specific priorities recognized under state law and other non-bankruptcy federal law.

Under California law, general assignments are created by agreement and not by the initiation of a court proceeding. Consequently, California general assignments do not create a public record and can typically be carried out more quickly than a court-supervised action (and can often avoid unwanted publicity).

The use of general assignments in California, as well as in many other states, has increased over the past several decades. In California, the debtor company and the prospective assignee may be located elsewhere but can designate that California law will apply.[1] This feature enables out-of-state assignors to choose the more favorable California law and its non-court supervised general assignments as a liquidation option.

Because general assignments have become more commonplace in California, this chapter will focus on California law but will at times refer to the law of other states when there are significant differences. For example, some states have more detailed statutory assignments that *do require* the instigation of

---

1   See Cal. Civ. Code §1646.5.

a court proceeding in connection with a general assignment or a sale of assets.[2]

A case in point involved an executive jet fuel company organized under Wyoming law that made a general assignment under California law. The company's facilities and creditors were not located in California, yet they completed a successful going-concern sale assignment. Likewise, a Pennsylvania data processing company made a general assignment under California law and also concluded a going concern sale, successfully.

The Parties to and Property of the General Assignment

The assignee. An assignee can be an individual or an entity (typically a corporation). The assignee acts for the assignor (the debtor company) and asserts claims to property coequal to but not more significant than the debtor. The assignee's job is to protect the assets of the estate and upon liquidation distribute the assets among the assignor's creditors according to priorities established by state law.

---

2 See 10 Del. C. §§7381 – 7387 (Delaware law requires, among other things, the filing of an inventory with the Register in Chancery); F.S.A. §§727.101 -727.117 (Florida law requires the filing of a petition with the state court); M.C.L.A. §§600.5201 – 600.5265 (Michigan law requires that assignees conduct an asset appraisal by two disinterested appraisers and the commencement of a court proceeding); M.S.A. §§577.11 – 577.18 (Minnesota law requires that the general assignment be filed with the state court); N.J.S.A. §§2A:19-1 – 2A:19-50 (New Jersey law requires that the assignment together with an inventory be filed in the public records); N.Y. Debt. & Cred. §§2 – 24 (New York law requires the commencement of a court proceeding to supervise general assignments); 39 P.S. §§39 – 96 (Assignments under Pennsylvania law are court supervised); V.T.C.A., Bus. & C. §§23.01-23.33 (Texas law does not require court supervision of general assignments, but does require an assignee to obtain a state court-approved bond).

The assignee *does not* assume the liabilities of the assignor's contractual agreements but does assume a fiduciary duty to the assignor's creditors to maintain the assets. As a result, the assignee must exercise ordinary caution and good faith in dealing with the assignor's contract obligations. If the assignee does not meet its fiduciary duty, it is liable for any losses.

An assignee may, in its discretion and the best interest of the creditors, choose to perform or decline to perform an assignor's part in an executory contract. (An executory contract requires performance on both sides of an agreement, such as supply agreement, a lease agreement, or a license agreement.) When an assignee induces another party to perform on a contract or otherwise obtains the benefit of a contract, the assignee must also assume that contract's obligations.

As a fiduciary to the assignor's creditors, the assignee assumes specific duties in the assignment estate's administration. Similar to a bankruptcy trustee, an assignee must liquidate the assignor's assets, equitably distribute the proceeds among the assignor's creditors, and provide an accounting to creditors within a reasonable time. An assignee is required to give notice of the assignment to all of the assignor's creditors and equity security holders and to establish a bar date by which the creditors may assert a claim against the assignor's assets.

Immediately upon taking a general assignment, the assignee will secure and inventory the assigned assets. (Sometimes the inventory count is concluded before the assignment occurs.) When inventories are significant, this may require either large in-house capabilities or outsourced assistance. All documentation must be preserved, including digital files.

If no sale process has been planned pre-assignment, once the assignee has inventoried and secured the debtor company's assets the sale process begins. Preparations may involve the services of a liquidator or private or public sale transaction, or the like. The timeline varies depending on the nature of the assignor's business and assets but, in most cases, it takes six months or less to complete the liquidation.

The assignor. The assignor may be a corporation, a limited liability company, an individual, a joint venture, or a partnership. The assignor's creditor claims are not discharged (legally released) in a general assignment, except for the payments that the assignee makes to creditors after liquidating the assets of the assignment estate. Therefore, in an individual case or a partnership or joint venture in which the partners are individuals, a general assignment is typically not advantageous.

Even though there is no discharge of liabilities, the effect of the notice to creditors of a general assignment that the assignor's business is no longer operating is likely to reduce, if not eliminate, creditor collection actions. Even so, however, because there is no discharge of liabilities, it would not be advisable for an assignor that is an entity to continue to operate when the assignment is complete.

The property. All property of the assignor, whether personal or real, must be assigned. In other words, the assignor cannot withhold specific assets from the assignment as a partial assignment. For a business entity, the assignment will include all property plus leasehold interests, lawsuits, legal claims, bank accounts, contract rights, and intellectual property, among others.

As to real property, a general assignment constitutes a conveyance under California law and is subject to all the recording provisions of the California Civil Code relating to real property transfers. When the assets include real property, the assignee must record an appropriate notice with the county recorder, which provides constructive notice of the assignment.

In protecting the assigned assets, the assignee in some states, such as California, is conferred with certain rights which are not available to the assignor. For example, the assignee may occupy the assignor's leased business premises for up to 90 days after the assignment commences, paying all rent due, even when a clause in the lease permits termination if the lessee becomes insolvent or an assignment occurs (which is typical). This right to occupy the assignor's business premises for a limited period enables the assignee to administer and liquidate the assignor's assets without fearing eviction from the premises.

Like a bankruptcy trustee, an assignee has legal standing to prosecute and defend claims against the assignor. The assignee is the legal representative of the assignor and, as a trustee for all the creditors, is "charged with the duty to defend the property in its hands against all unjust adverse claims." However, an assignee acquires no greater property rights than what the assignor possessed at the time of the assignment.

Assignee's Recovery Powers

An assignee can avoid or recover certain transfers for the benefit of the assignor's creditors. Just as in a chapter 7 bankruptcy, these avoidance or recovery claims augment the assignment estate and increase the potential recovery for the creditors.

In California, the assignee is conferred with a special standing to prosecute and recover certain property transfers for the benefit of the creditors if they are made within 90 days of a general assignment and prefer specific creditors. (While it is beyond the scope of this discussion, some argue that an assignee's avoidance actions are preempted by the bankruptcy code.[3])

To avoid (or recover) a preferential property transfer in California, the assignee must prove that

- the assignor transferred to or for the benefit of a creditor;

- the transfer was on account of a pre-existing debt owed before the transfer was made;

- the transfer was made while the assignor was insolvent;

- the transfer was made within 90 days before making the general assignment, unless the creditor is an insider (an officer, director, or partner) and has reasonable cause to believe that the assignor was insolvent at the time of the transfer, and the transfer occurred between 90 days and one year of the assignment; and

- the transfer enabled the creditor to receive more than another creditor of the same class (for example, unsecured creditors are usually classed together).

Note: By definition, a company is insolvent when its balance sheet has more debts than assets. An assignee must take action to recover preferences within one year after the making of the general assignment.

---

3 See Weinberg, Joel B. "California General Assignments: Still Alive, Kicking, and Useful." *California Bankruptcy Journal*, vol. 29, no. 2 (2007).

The California preference statute contains similar exceptions to those in section 547(c) of the bankruptcy code, which discusses defenses to preference avoidance. Some of those exceptions include

- a concurrent exchange for new value given to the assignor;

- a transfer made in the ordinary course of business of the assignor and the transferee;

- an enabling loan exception; and

- the new value exception.

In addition to preference recoveries, and similar to a bankruptcy trustee, an assignee may recover other avoidable transfers. California law provides for two types of avoidable transfers:

(1) an "actual" avoidable transfer, a transfer made with the intent to hinder, delay, or defraud any creditor of the assignor; and

(2) a "constructive" avoidable transfer, a transfer made without receiving reasonably equivalent value in exchange.

An example of the former is when a company in dire financial straits transfers a piece of machinery to a related company for little or no consideration, with the specific purpose of removing that asset from creditor claims. An example of the latter is when an asset is transferred without adequate consideration, even without proof of intent to remove it from creditors.

Transfers of personal property without immediate delivery or change of property possession are also avoidable by an assignee. For example, if the assignor seeks to transfer assets, such as equipment, to another party but the equipment remains at the same location, it may give rise to the assignee's ability to recover those transferred assets unless the transferor records a notice with the secretary of state.

An assignee may also, as under the bankruptcy code, set aside or avoid a security interest in personal property that is not perfected following the required legal process. Under the Uniform Commercial Code, which is substantially the same in all states, a credit provider, such as a bank lender or an equipment financer, will secure its claim by entering into an agreement with the borrower and filing a UCC-1 form with the secretary of state of the state in which the business is incorporated. There are a significant number of complex rules that need to be followed to create and perfect a security interest, and if there is a failure by the credit provider to comply with the perfection rules, the assignee, like a bankruptcy trustee, may set aside the security interest. The effect of doing so is that the credit provider, who otherwise would have a first right to those assets, is now treated as any other unsecured creditor.

Examples of deficiencies arise from time to time in some universal fact patterns. The creditor may have filed the financing statement in the jurisdiction of the company's headquarters or where its major facilities are located, instead of the state of the company's formation, as required by law. Or sometimes there is a failure to file a continuation statement before the initial financing statement lapses after five years. A continuation statement that is timely filed allows the secured creditor to secure the assets for a further five years.

In other cases, the issue arises when a debtor holds inventory under a consignment arrangement but the vendor has failed to file a financing statement to document its consignment. Generally, when goods are sold on consignment, the consignor retains title to the goods until they are sold by the consignee to the consignee's customers, at which time title passes to the customer and the consignor is to be paid. The Uniform Commercial Code requires that the consignor file a statement with the secretary of state to put third parties on notice that the goods in the possession of the consignee really belong to the consignor. Consignors often fail to file this notice. In this event, the assignee may prevail over the consignor-vendor.

Sometimes liquidation is prompted because a creditor brings a lawsuit and obtains an attachment on the company's assets. This typically occurs well before the date that the lawsuit goes to trial. In an attachment, the creditor makes an application to persuade the court of its likelihood of success at trial, and if certain other conditions are met, the court may order that defendant's assets should be seized and held pending trial. If granted by the court, the attachment locks up the company's assets and can put a company out of business. If the attachment occurs within 90 days of the general assignment, it may be set aside by the assignee.

If a creditor attempts to seize the assets of the assignor after an assignment, this too may be set aside by an assignee on the basis that title to all assets had already passed to the assignee upon the assignment. At this point, any lawsuit against the assignor company is merely a lawsuit against a shell entity with no assets.

Distribution and Priorities

Similar to bankruptcy cases, state law provides for certain priorities in the distribution of assignment estate. While the federal bankruptcy code is clear regarding those priorities, some state law equivalents are less clear.

California law establishes the following priority-of-distribution scheme for the assets of an assignment:

- Secured creditors, who receive their collateral or its value.

- Debts due to the United States, including tax debts. This priority is more extensive than would be the case under the bankruptcy code. For example, breach of contract claims between the assignor and the U.S. would have priority in an assignment, but would not have that priority in a bankruptcy.

- Allowed claims for wages, salaries, or commissions. including vacation, severance, and sick leave pay earned by individuals, but only to the extent of $4,300 for each, earned within 90 days before the date of assignment. In contrast to bankruptcy, a California assignment for benefit of creditors creates a *lien*, and not merely a priority, on the property assigned in favor of wage claimants of the assignor, which is superior in entitlement to expenses of administration. These labor liens, as opposed to mere priority claims, could potentially wipe out the assignee's ability to be compensated for the costs of administering the estate, which otherwise would have a senior priority.

- Allowed claims for contributions to any employee benefit plans, generally arising from services rendered within 180 days before the assignment, to the extent of $4,300 per employee.

- Delinquent state taxes, including interest and penalties for sales and use taxes, income taxes, and bank and corporate taxes.

- Unsecured creditors' claims arising from deposits of up to $900 for the purchase, lease, or rental of property or the purchase of services for personal, family, or household use of such persons that were not delivered or provided.

- Unpaid unemployment insurance contributions, including interest and penalties.

- The State of California, for all money owed for the sale of licenses and license tags.

- General unsecured claims filed in a timely manner.

Rarely in a general assignment are assets sufficient to pay all unsecured creditors the full principal amount of their respective claims. However, if there are sufficient assets, unsecured creditors would typically be entitled to payment of both principal and interest. Any surplus is held in trust by the assignee and returned to the assignor after creditors who did not participate have had an opportunity to reach the surplus.

Facilitating the Sale of a Business through a General Assignment

One of the principal benefits of an assignment is the ability to facilitate a sale of the assignor's assets. As noted in chapter 8 of this book, a buyer of distressed assets is typically concerned about whether the purchase of assets carries with it any of the liabilities of the seller. Therefore, buyers often seek to structure the transaction through various legal means to insulate the buyer from the seller's liabilities, other than those the buyer has contractually assumed. An assignment is an effective way of structuring such a sale.

Like a sale under the federal bankruptcy code, a general assignment can facilitate the transition of financially distressed business assets to a buyer, while preserving the going-concern value of the assets and achieving a greater recovery for creditors. Since assignees generally do not operate the business of the assignor, these types of transactions are typically structured *before* the making of the general assignment. The assignor remains in control and possession of the company's assets until actually making the assignment and, immediately after that, closing the sale transaction.

In this regard, the assignee's experience and reputation are critical in several respects. First, an experienced assignee is better equipped to plan for and deal with potential and actual issues that arise, and will maximize the prospect that the transaction will actually close. Second, the assignee's reputation can be critical in gaining the confidence of creditors and of the court in the event that an involuntary bankruptcy petition is filed (see below).

Due diligence commences when a potential assignee is selected. The extent and value of the assignor's assets is a critical part of this inquiry. The assignor's tangible and intangible personal property and any real property interests will be valued, and a search will be conducted for security interests, including filed financing statements, filings with the department of motor vehicles, real property records, copyright mortgages, similar filings against patents and trademarks, and other encumbrances. If the assignor's business is in any way related to food production or consumption, the assignor's trade payables must be carefully scrutinized for possible trust claims, as federal law provides specific legal priorities for sellers of perishable commodities. The prospective assignee must also assess the exposure of the assignor's assets in the marketplace. For example, has the assignor previously retained a broker or investment banker to market the assets?

After the initial investigation, the potential assignee then determines an appropriate strategy for selling the assets as a going concern. In some cases, the assignor has already identified a buyer. Whether the assignee proceeds with that buyer will depend on several factors, including

- the present condition of the assignor's business and whether it can sustain continued operations pending further marketing efforts;

- the degree to which the identified buyer is the result of comprehensive marketing efforts;

- the degree to which the price and terms offered by the buyer differ from the appraised values; and

- whether the buyer is affiliated with the assignor or its insiders.

If the potential assignee rejects the identified buyer, an appropriate marketing strategy for the particular circumstances is developed, for example, a public auction of the assets as a going concern. If the assignee determines that a public auction is the best approach, the selection of the auctioneer, in some instances, is determined through a competitive bid.

Certain buyer protections, such as a reasonable "breakup fee," to compensate the initial offeror for its due diligence and legal costs, are also considered. (A discussion of breakup fees in connection with bankruptcy sale transactions is discussed in chapter 8 of this book, and a similar process can be used in a sale under an assignment.)

During the marketing phase, lawyers will prepare the purchase and sale documents and other related documents, such as subordination agreements, consents, and the like, for the potential assignee and will negotiate with secured creditors. Typically, secured creditors holding properly perfected security interests or liens receive payment from the sale proceeds. In some instances, a secured creditor will consent to the transfer of the assignor's assets subject to its security interest, to the buyer.

If in connection with the sale transaction with the assignee, the buyer also seeks to obtain the benefit of agreements with third parties, such as licensors of intellectual property or lessors of real or personal property, the buyer must negotiate suitable agreements directly with those third parties. There is no basis under California assignment law to mandate that the third-party licensors are compelled to assign their licenses to the buyer. This is one of the significant differences to federal bankruptcy law, which under certain circumstances will permit a debtor-seller to assume and assign an ongoing contract or an unexpired lease to a third-party buyer of the debtor's assets, even without the consent of the other contracting party.

The sale process culminates with a targeted sale date, which is often the date of the making of the general assignment. The assignor continues to operate the business until the assignment date, then immediately transfers assets through the going-concern sale, and the buyer runs the company the next day with little or no interruption. The making of the general assignment and the closing of the sale transaction occur almost simultaneously. The assignor makes the general assignment, and then the assignee, as the seller, executes the purchase and sale agreement.

While consent of general unsecured creditors is not required in some instances, such as a sale to insiders or to an entity in which insiders have an interest, an assignee may call a meeting of creditors and, following appropriate disclosure, obtain their vote before concluding the sale. If the assignee does not elect to call a meeting of creditors because it is either impractical or resisted by the assignor, the prospective assignee must ensure that the assignor's creditors will receive at least as much from a sale of the assets to the related-party buyer as they would have received from a sale to an unrelated third-party. The value paid by a related buyer must be at least equal to or greater than market value for the assets being acquired.

Upon closing the transaction, the assignment proceeds in a similar manner as any liquidation. The assignee notifies creditors who file their claims with the assignment estate. The assignee also pursues any preferences and avoidance-power actions, and liquidates other claims that constitute property of the assignment trust. Finally, the assignee distributes creditor proceeds.

Effect of Bankruptcy Proceedings

If a creditor is dissatisfied with a general assignment, it may choose to file an involuntary bankruptcy petition against the assignor. Indeed, the bankruptcy code provides that a general assignment for the benefit of creditors is itself grounds for an involuntary case in bankruptcy.[4]

Even though a general assignment for the benefit of creditors is grounds for filing an involuntary bankruptcy, courts may refrain from ordering the involuntary bankruptcy "if another forum is available to protect the interests of both parties, or if there is a pending proceeding in a state court (e.g., assignment for benefit of creditors)."

One significant factor leading a court to abstain is the existence of a nonfederal insolvency proceeding that has progressed so far as to make a bankruptcy duplicative and costly, such as an assignment for the benefit of creditors. However, some courts will permit the involuntary bankruptcy whereby creditors could exercise powers under the bankruptcy code which are unavailable under state law.

When a reputable assignee is in place and administration of the general assignment has commenced, courts are often willing to dismiss an involuntary petition.

In one such case, an assignee had marketed a company's assets on a going-concern basis. The company imported, finished, and sold stone, such as granite and marble. An institutional lender had a secured claim of approximately $20 million and was willing to take a "short pay" of roughly $8 million on a sale to a third-party buyer, because the value of all company assets (which were also the lender's collateral) was significantly

---

4 In *re Mineral Hill Corp.*, 16 B.R. 687, 688 (Bankr. D. Md. 1982).

less than the amount owed to the lender. Eleven creditors joined in an involuntary bankruptcy petition that was filed against the company after the general assignment commenced and the sale had concluded. The assignee then filed a motion to dismiss the petition. The court ruled in favor of the assignee, noting that liquidation through bankruptcy would not accomplish more than that of the general assignment. The court deferred to the state–law-authorized assignment that had preceded the involuntary bankruptcy petition.

As this example demonstrates, creditors need to be cautious before filing an involuntary bankruptcy. If the court rules against them, it may also require the petitioning creditors to bear the costs of the debtor and assignee in defending an involuntary petition upon dismissal. On the other hand, if a bankruptcy court does permit the involuntary bankruptcy to proceed, the court may order the assignee to turn over the assignor's property to the bankruptcy trustee, in which case the assignee must file an accounting with that trustee.

Conclusion

General assignments remain a viable tool for liquidating the assets of a distressed business. As a practical matter, general assignments are an alternative to bankruptcy when the situation does not require the coercive powers of the U.S. Bankruptcy Code, such as the automatic stay and the power to assume and assign executory contracts and unexpired leases. General assignments can be less costly and are often more expeditious than liquidation under chapter 7. Consequently, any decision to liquidate a business entity should consider a state-law general assignment for the benefit of creditors.

— ◇ —

Joel B. Weinberg is an adjunct professor of law at Loyola Law School and chief executive officer of Insolvency Services Group, Inc., an entity which serves as an assignee for the benefit of creditors. Having begun his career as a corporate and tax lawyer, for more than 30 years Mr. Weinberg has specialized in commercial bankruptcy and debt restructuring work. A special thanks to William Shafton, Esq., for his meaningful contribution to this chapter. Contact Mr. Weinberg at jweinberg@usisg.com.

10

Out-of-Court
Debt Restructuring

By Chuck Klaus

O ut-of-court debt restructuring, often referred to as an out-of-court workout, is a viable alternative to chapter 11 bankruptcy for many financially distressed companies. Without resorting to court intervention, a company may be able to reorganize itself in less time and with less expense. In addition, there likely will be less operational disruption and reduced public exposure of confidential business matters. For a financially troubled company, an out-of-court debt restructuring should be evaluated as an option before resorting to bankruptcy.

— ◇ —

Out-of-Court Debt Restructuring vs. Bankruptcy

While it may sound counterintuitive, some companies can't afford bankruptcy. The cost to obtain funding, pay all the necessary professionals, and know with reasonable certainty that a company will emerge and perform successfully after bankruptcy can be prohibitive.

Alternatives are neither easy nor foolproof. Bringing a company out of financial distress in an out-of-court debt restructuring is not without significant challenges. In some situations, reorganization in bankruptcy may be preferable.

If a debtor operates numerous retail locations and the restructuring program targets several for closure, in bankruptcy the debtor is entitled to reject or terminate a lease. A rejection during the bankruptcy is treated as a breach of the lease occurring immediately before the bankruptcy. The landlord may file a breach-of-lease claim, which becomes an unsecured claim and is classed together with other general unsecured claims and is usually paid only a percent-on-the-dollar, saving the bankruptcy estate much-needed funds. Also, bankruptcy places a cap on landlord breach-of-lease damages, whereas an out-of-court workout does not. Bankruptcy provides for a cap on rent based upon the greater of 15 percent of the remaining lease term of the lease or one year.

If the debtor company is a licensee of intellectual property and expects to sell those licenses as part of its restructuring, bankruptcy law, in certain circumstances, permits a licensee to assume and assign those licenses to a third-party buyer, even over the licensor's objection. In an out-of-court restructuring, the debtor must get the licensor's approval to assign assets.

When real property lease rejections or license sales are not an issue, creditors often prefer that the debtor attempt an informal out-of-court debt restructuring over bankruptcy. Mainly because there are cost savings, but also because the odds of achieving a successful reorganization improve when both debtor and creditor are working together to achieve a common goal.

If debtor and creditors can avoid the strong-arm powers of the bankruptcy court in order to achieve the same result with significantly less cost, it is wise to attempt an out-of-court restructuring.

A debtor's credibility with its creditors is a significant component of fostering cooperation among creditors in a restructuring. Deploying a neutral third party to administer the process and act as an intermediary between the financially challenged debtor and its creditors increases the chance of a favorable outcome. This chapter details the specific mechanics of the out-of-court restructuring process, along with some personal experiences working with well over 200 financially troubled companies.

First Signs of Financial Trouble and What to Do

As a general rule, owners of companies and current management are very competent when it comes to industry knowledge and sales. However, they are often weak in collecting receivables, and even worse in reacting to changes in the marketplace that lead to negative cash-flow issues. Failure to recognize the signs of financial trouble can reduce the possibility of success.

In executing a turnaround, the urgency of a cash shortage combined with the necessity to improve the business's fundamentals creates an intense environment. The company typically needs breathing room. When signs of financial trouble first appear, management should secure professional advice from those in the insolvency or turnaround management industries to analyze the troubled company and make recommendations.

Management often will be forced to make some very tough decisions throughout the turnaround process, such as

downsizing overhead and reducing labor, eliminating less profitable products or services, and restructuring debt. Owners and
managers who get ahead of the problems and solicit professionals to handle the many facets of distress are then able to focus
on essential business operations and customers, and protect
much-needed revenue streams.

In the early stages of financial distress, management's
advisers need to initiate communications with the company's
creditors, including the secured lender(s) and trade creditors.
Honest and open conversations will help to restore creditor
confidence and bolster company creditability. Creditors are
typically aware of the impact that bankruptcy will have on both
the company and on them, and will respect the company that
works to improve its business prospects while an experienced
professional—a neutral third party—pursues creditor cooperation and conducts negotiations.

The business will also need a rebuilding strategy, which
involves developing a business plan to reorganize the company
from the top down. The program should begin with a pro forma
cash flow and income statement, based on cost-cutting assumptions and other measures necessary to return the company to
positive cash flow. (See the detailed discussion on turnaround
accounting in chapter 5 of this book.)

Often, one or more competitors may have an interest in
acquiring the company. For companies in financial distress,
sometimes those discussions do not materialize into any meaningful offer once the potential acquirer starts its due diligence
and learns of the company's serious economic issues and the
cost to rehabilitate the company. Likewise, the company may
have serious concerns about disclosing its financial matters to
a competitor. For example, unless the troubled company has a
unique product, technology, or niche in the market that would

motivate a strategic partner to spend good money after bad, it is may be wiser not to reveal the troubled financial position to the marketplace. With such knowledge, competitors may wait until assets can be bought for pennies on the dollar in an assignment for the benefit of creditors or bankruptcy proceeding.

Mechanics of an Out-of-Court Reorganization

Success in an out-of-court workout depends on management's ability to convince creditors that the company will become profitable again or that it has a potential exit strategy with one or more strategic companies that will generate a better outcome for creditors than a forced liquidation sale.

Part of the process involved in convincing creditors to stick with the troubled company will require cutting costs. As management attempts to facilitate reorganization or promote a sale discussion with strategic competitors or other parties who are interested in acquiring some or all company assets, it must also devote significant time and energy to implementing cost-cutting measures. Because the company's turnaround or exit strategy is dependent on the cooperation of the creditors in an out-of-court reorganization, engaging a neutral advisor with financial and turnaround management experience is critical for several reasons. First, the advisor will analyze the financial condition of the company and prepare a plan of organization based on actual data and projections. Second, the advisor will meet with the company's creditors to present that plan, encourage cooperation, and negotiate as needed.

Several caveats are in play during the process. Creditors are already owed money and may lose patience if management requests a forbearance while at the same time asking for creditors' continued support in supplying needed products or services. In this scenario, creditors may doubt the company's sincerity and ability to affect a viable turnaround strategy. The neutral third party is key. It is his or her job, along with company management, to outline an acceptable plan for rebuilding the company and present it, convincingly, to unsecured trade creditors. The debtor enhances its potential to restore credibility and obtain creditor cooperation with accurate financial information and a practical plan in place.

The Meeting of Creditors

The purpose of the meeting of creditors is to explain the current financial condition of the company, including what led up to the financial crisis and the overall plan to reorganize the company and return it to profitability. Statistically, only about 30 percent of the creditors (by dollar amount) attend a scheduled creditor meeting, typically those holding the highest debt. Management should notify its largest and most essential creditors by phone before the notice of the creditor meeting is sent. The call will explain the purpose of the meeting and invite them to serve on the creditors' committee. The turnaround professionals engaged by the company can also assist in this regard. Secured creditors, such as bank lenders, are not invited to the meeting, as it is only a meeting of the *unsecured* creditors.

Typically, management doesn't provide specific financial information at this point. The focus is to present creditors with a high-level plan to get some breathing room. Creditors will need to agree to cooperate before being given confidential financial information.

After the presentation, counsel for the debtor company will explain that without the cooperation of the unsecured creditors, the company may be forced to liquidate or go into a bankruptcy reorganization, which may delay the reorganization process and add significantly more costs compared to the out-of-court process. Counsel will point out that the company's unsecured creditors will ultimately bear these costs.

After a question and answer session, counsel for the company will invite the creditors to form an advisory committee to represent the interests of all of the general unsecured creditors in monitoring management's efforts to reorganize the company back to profitability. The committee also guides the negotiations with the debtor regarding the plan of reorganization to repay creditors. Counsel will ask that creditors agree to hold their debt in abeyance for 90 days while the process begins to take shape, which period can be extended or terminated at the recommendation of the committee. Counsel will inform creditors that the company will continue to trade with their existing creditors on a cash basis, as long as price, quality, and service remain competitive.

Creditors' Committee

Everyone benefits when a company survives and, therefore, forming a creditors' committee to work with management on its plan of reorganization is optimal. Typically, larger or more interested creditors volunteer to serve. The committee will schedule periodic conference calls with the debtor company for updates and will send out occasional communications to the general creditor body regarding its progress in working toward a plan of reorganization. As time goes on, the creditors' committee will give its recommendation to continue or terminate the moratorium, based on what they determine to be in the best interests of the creditors.

In particular, the creditors' committee cannot bind creditors to any repayment plan. However, because parties who are willing to donate their time to serve on an advisory creditors' committee would be among the largest creditors and have a vested interest in seeing the company survive for everyone's benefit, their decisions and recommendations carry a lot of weight with the general creditor body.

The creditors' committee should retain counsel for purposes of legal guidance and drafting committee bylaws, as well as working with the committee members in negotiating a formal composition agreement. Although there is a cost to the company to engage in this process, including paying legal fees to the committee counsel, it is usually significantly less than the cost of a bankruptcy proceeding.

Grant of Security Interest

To help ensure that recalcitrant unsecured creditors do not take action to derail an out-of-court workout, often there is a grant of a security interest to the third-party workout facilitator on behalf of the unsecured creditors. Unlike bankruptcy, there is no automatic stay in an out-of-court reorganization that precludes creditors from either filing a lawsuit(s) during the out-of-court process or continuing to prosecute existing litigation. Because there is no automatic stay in an out-of-court reorganization, the granting of a security interest in the assets of the debtor for the benefit of all unsecured creditors acts as an equalizer that discourages creditors from initiating or incurring additional costs to continue prosecuting existing litigation.

The grant of the security interest (that may be junior to existing liens) on all assets of the debtor precludes any creditor from receiving preference over another. In essence, the creditor lien protects the assets from any creditor's trying to levy upon or gain an advantage over another creditor through litigation by attempting a writ of attachment or placing a judgment lien against the assets of the debtor. In almost all cases, the liquidation value of the assets is insufficient to satisfy the lien of the secured creditor (assuming that there is such a lender), leaving nothing available for the general unsecured creditors. The granting of a junior lien in favor of all unsecured creditors thus acts as an effective equalizer for all general unsecured claims. Because the creditor lien is typically held in trust by the third-party administrator at the direction of the creditors' committee, it can be used to defeat any attempt by an aggressive creditor who decides to attempt to levy on the assets of the debtor during the pendency of the out-of-court reorganization process.

The following example demonstrates the effectiveness of granting such a security interest. During an out-of-court workout, a creditor with a claim for $60,000 filed a lawsuit together with an application for a writ of attachment, attempting to seize assets of the debtor to satisfy its unsecured claim. One of the allegations of the creditor trying to seize assets was that the granting of the lien to the general unsecured creditors was a fraudulent transfer, as the transfer lacked sufficient consideration. (See chapter 1 for a discussion of fraudulent transfers.) Although the court, in this case, did not issue a published decision, it deemed that the moratorium on the antecedent debt was sufficient consideration for the grant of the security interest. The court upheld the grant of the security interest and denied the application for the attachment lien.

Composition Agreement

The ultimate objective of the out-of-court workout is to reach an agreement with creditors regarding the repayment program of the debtor company. The composition agreement, or repayment plan, will vary depending on the composition of creditors and other issues, such as lawsuits, pending claims, and the negotiations between the debtor company and the creditors' committee. Because Since the creditors' committee cannot bind creditors to the repayment plan, approval of any composition agreement usually requires that at least 90 percent of the creditors—in dollar amount—consent to the plan. The debtor company can accept or modify the 90 percent requirement based upon the composition of consents.

Sometimes a small percentage of creditors do not return ballots. To deal with this issue, a composition agreement might have an "accord and satisfaction" provision added. Accord and satisfaction is a state law concept that imposes a new agreement based on the giving and receiving of consideration that is different from, usually less than, the underlying agreement. The accord-and-satisfaction law holds that if a creditor fails to return its ballot, the plan deems those creditors to have accepted the plan. Thus, any creditor who does not reject the plan, receives notice of payment under the plan, and cashes that payment cannot later claim that it never agreed to the plan. Any such creditor subjects itself to the legal argument that an accord and satisfaction exist between the two parties and that the creditor is bound to the terms and conditions of the repayment plan.

Composition agreements often require that creditors agree to discount their claims, which are paid out over time in monthly or quarterly installments. In these agreements, the third-party administrator acts as a disbursing agent in accordance with the creditors' terms and conditions. In out-of-court repayment plans, the creditors' committee coordinates with the debtor to negotiate the best repayment agreement, based on projected net profits, which establishes the manner and timing of payments to creditors. The debtor submits its repayment plan to the committee first, based on cash-flow projections and other assumptions that the creditors' committee needs to analyze, similar to a disclosure statement that creditors would see in a formal bankruptcy plan.

Also similar to a bankruptcy case, creditors are separated into various classes of claim, depending on priority and size. For instance, it is very prevalent to form a convenience class of claims comprising creditors owed nominal amounts. The convenience class is paid first, up to the set limit; for example, $5,000. Other creditors might also want to take advantage of these terms and reduce their claims to $5,000 each. The rationale for forming a convenience class is for administrative convenience. Because the 80/20 rule generally applies, i.e., 80 percent of the debt is held by 20 percent of the creditors, it is administratively efficient to satisfy small claims first.

The second class of unsecured creditors might consist of those with claims over $5,000 but less than $25,000. This class may receive payment of some cents on the dollar over a period. The timing of those payments would start after the convenience class is paid in full.

Finally, class-three creditors are those with claims greater than $25,000, who are generally offered a greater percentage on the dollar than class two, but may have to defer payment under the plan until class-one and class-two creditors have been satisfied. The success of the out-of-court workouts lies in the fact that the creditors' committee and debtor company negotiate a repayment plan before creditors receive it and take a vote.

Using an Out-of-Court Reorganization Process for a Pre-Packaged Bankruptcy

There are times when a formal bankruptcy will be needed and an out-of-court workout will not suffice; for example, a need for an automatic stay, to void involuntary liens, or to sell assets free and clear of liens. These are only available through bankruptcy. However, sometimes the debtor company will want to formulate a plan with creditors before the actual filing of the bankruptcy case.

Here a similar process can be used to call a meeting of creditors to form a creditors' committee in anticipation of filing chapter 11 under the bankruptcy code. The objective here is to form a creditors' committee that can review aspects of the proposed chapter 11 plan, including, for example, a potential offer to acquire assets of the debtor that would be subject to overbid and bankruptcy court approval. This process can be used to help formulate a "prepackaged bankruptcy" that will enable the debtor company to move through the bankruptcy case much more quickly, thereby reducing bankruptcy fees and costs. The value that the prepackaged process offers is that a lot of the legwork can be completed pre-bankruptcy by a creditors' committee comprising the more significant creditors who, under a confidentiality agreement, can review the proposed transaction to determine the support of the committee in a bankruptcy filing.

The members of the pre-bankruptcy committee will typically become members of the committee in the bankruptcy case, with some minor additions or modifications. By working through all of the problematic issues and having a firm plan in place before bankruptcy, the debtor, with the support of the creditors' committee, can move through the bankruptcy case far more efficiently. Forming a pre-bankruptcy committee is another example of using the out-of-court reorganization process even if the intention is to file bankruptcy subsequently.

Preference Recoveries

Finally, any discussion of the out-of-court reorganization process would not be complete without discussing preferential transfers. As noted in chapter 1, preferences are payments made to creditors within 90 days of a bankruptcy filing or payments made to insiders within one year of a bankruptcy filing. These payments may be recoverable in a formal bankruptcy proceeding if made outside the ordinary course of business. Of course, an out-of-court workout is not a formal bankruptcy, and so these recovery rights do not exist, and it thus may appear that this inquiry is irrelevant. However, even in an out-of-court workout, this information must be disclosed to the creditors' committee. This, understandably, may give management of the debtor some cause for concern, specifically if insiders of the debtor company were the recipients of such preferential payments.

While the creditors' committee must look at all transfers that may be preferential in nature, typically unless the transfers are sufficiently large, it is doubtful that the creditors' committee would take action to promote a bankruptcy filing simply to recover these transfers. Rather, more often in these situations, the creditors' committee concludes that leaving the company in the out-of-court process exceeds any perceived potential benefit that forcing the company into bankruptcy to preserve any recovery of preferential transfers would afford.

Conclusion

The out-of-court reorganization process works best when a disinterested third party is contracted to provide a forum in which
the financially distressed company can meet with its creditors
to reorganize its business affairs outside of court supervision.
More often than not this process is successful but, of course, the
out-of-court workout process can fail or it may not be advisable.

Even when the process begins as an out-of-court workout and later becomes a bankruptcy, unsecured creditors are
likely in a much better situation, having been secured as a result
of the prior grant of the security interest. Also, they are fully
informed, thereby being able to avoid preference pitfalls in a
bankruptcy. The following example highlights such a case.

A company in the entertainment industry was involved
in an out-of-court reorganization that lasted almost two years
without the debtor's being able to achieve profitability sufficient to fund a repayment plan. At the time that the out-of-
court workout process began, unsecured creditors were given
a lien in trust, and vendors started dealing with the company
on a COD basis. Creditors received information along the way.
Unfortunately, the company's revenues deteriorated over time,
ultimately forcing management to cease business operations.

When the news broke, the creditors' committee was not
surprised. Even though the workout was not successful over
the duration of the out-of-court process, the creditors had been
kept informed of progress and traded with the company on a
COD basis. As a result, the creditors mainly had offset their
losses from profits that they would not have realized had the
company shut down from day one. The case illustrates that
creditors usually support the out-of-court reorganization process, as they have nothing to lose at that point and everything

to gain. In particular, with an experienced third party to facilitate, it can be a win-win process for all parties.

— ◇ —

Chuck Klaus has more than 25 years of experience acting as a fiduciary, specializing in the liquidation of business assets through general assignments for the benefit of creditors, in addition to attempts to restructure troubled companies in out-of-court restructuring plans. Mr. Klaus has also served as chief responsible officer in bankruptcy court appointments and state court receiverships, and as a provisional director in state court litigation matters. In addition to being a licensed auctioneer and a certified personal property appraiser, he has conducted or managed over 100 public auctions for commercial banks, asset based lenders, bankruptcy trustees, and private equity and venture capital lenders.

Contact him at chuck@abcservices.group.

CHAPTER

11

Receiverships

By Stephen J. Donell

Financially troubled companies are often subject to creditor pressures to force bankruptcy for debt recovery. But for many companies, bankruptcy should be a last resort. A distressed business may have a viable alternative.

In some instances, a company may be able to restructure its debt, bring in new capital, or modify operations to respond to increasing pressure from its creditors. Often these actions can be developed by the company's professional restructuring team: its CPAs, attorneys, and financial consultants. The advantages of this approach can be significant, as the company itself largely controls the restructuring, often achieving positive outcomes, fewer disruptions, and less cost. But in receivership, the situation is reversed.

A receivership is a court action *imposed* upon a company, often with minimal warning, and without the company's consent, control, or input. In a receivership, a non-related individual or entity is appointed to take custody and manage the company for a period, to preserve money, property, or other assets that are subject to litigation. When the court issues a final judgment in connection with the underlying litigation, the receiver's job is to ensure that assets remain available to accomplish what has been ordered by the court.

Receivership is not usually a welcome event for management. Although a wide variety of circumstances exist, generally the appointment of a receiver over a company will result in the principals' loss of control, damage to the company's reputation, and even the liquidation of all company assets.

However, it is not in every instance that receivership results in such negative consequences. The nature of the case, the initial reason(s) for the receiver's appointment, and the overall level of cooperation afforded to the receiver by the company's principals and employees will materially impact receivership outcomes. At the very least, receivership administration offers flexibility and customization.

Even though receivership is not the usual turnaround process, receiverships can and do occur in financially distressed businesses, and management needs to understand how they work and what to expect if a receiver is appointed. Because receiverships are usually an unwelcome event for management, management may often seek to forestall a receiver by filing bankruptcy.

— ◇ —

Receivership Basics

Receiverships as a legal remedy began hundreds of years ago in medieval English courts. Peter Davidson aptly describes the basics in his book *Ask The Receiver* (Davidson Press, 2014): "A receiver is an agent and an officer of the court which acts on behalf of the court. All receivership estate assets and property, pursuant to the order appointing receiver, under the receiver's custody and control is *in custodia legis*—in the custody of the court."

A receiver is usually an individual; however, sometimes a company is appointed as receiver. A party nominates a receiver, and a court appoints the receiver. To act as a receiver requires no particular qualifications, such as a license or professional designation. Instead, the appointing court will carefully review the background, education, and experience of the proposed receiver to ensure that the nominated receiver has the requisite expertise to fulfill the duties and obligations ordered by the court.

Authority. While the statutory basis for a receiver's appointment varies from state to state, it is common that courts have the power to appoint receivers solely based on their general equitable authority. Some states have a very extensive body of law addressing receiverships, while others do not. A federal court under the applicable United States code may also appoint a receiver. However, the federal district court must have jurisdiction to do so.

Neutrality. For most receivership matters, the proposed receiver must be neutral. Some states even have mandatory disclosure requirements for the receiver to affirm neutrality. For example, a receiver under consideration as an appointed receiver must make a complete disclosure regarding any financial or other ties to that company and any parties involved in the litigation. Parties and the court will review all such relationships and may preclude the receiver's appointment.

Powers and duties. The receiver's powers and duties are established and identified in the order "appointing receiver." If the moving party can establish the urgency, such as to prevent a loss or removal of an asset, a receiver may be appointed by the court on an emergency, or *ex parte* basis, with a later hearing to confirm the appointment of the receiver.

The court can grant a receiver expansive and broad powers, including the following:

- To assume full control of defendants in the receivership, including the ability to hire and fire all employees

- To take exclusive custody, control, and possession of all company assets and documents, wherever located, including all tangible personal property such as records, documents, computers, bank accounts, accounts receivables, contracts, and cash

- To redirect mail to the receiver's office

- To take physical possession of the business location, including the ability to change locks, security codes, and access devices

- To continue to conduct the business over receivership defendants or to liquidate defendant assets

In addition, the order appointing receiver will often include a temporary restraining order and asset freeze to restrain all defendants, successors, assigns, officers, agents, servants, employees, independent contractors, and other identified persons from, among other things, selling, liquidating, assigning, encumbering, or converting company assets. The receiver has virtually complete control over every aspect of the distressed business in receivership and is vested with enormous power.

Receivership Appointments

Receiverships can be appointed in both civil and criminal legal actions and are a provisional, or interim, remedy and not a cause of action. In other words, one cannot sue to have a receiver appointed; there must be existing, underlying litigation. However, in limited circumstances, such as in California, a receiver may be sought to dissolve a corporation without underlying litigation.

A court may appoint a receiver for a variety of reasons, including legal actions involving

- foreclosure of real property;

- enforcement of judgment;

- allegations of fraud or deceptive business practices;

- breach of contract or fiduciary duty, or fraudulent transfer;

- divorce;

- corporate dissolution;

- government enforcement cases, including state agencies and federal agencies such as the Securities and Exchange Commission, the Federal Trade Commission and Commodity Futures Trading Commission; and

- enforcement of statutory and contractual rights by secured lenders, shareholders, or partners.

Receivership actions commonly fall into one of two distinct types. The first type appoints a "limited purpose" receiver to take possession of, preserve, and maintain the collateral for a loan, such as a rents and profits receiver when real estate is involved. The limited purpose receiver in a real estate action has a very particular purpose; for example, to provide the lender access or to perform an environmental report or appraisal.

The second type appoints an "equity" receiver over the defendant debtor, not just the defendant or borrower's assets. Allegations of mismanagement, fraud, or improper acts typically trigger this type of action.

The nature of the dispute determines where to file the case; whether in federal or state court. When a party nominates a receiver, either through a noticed motion or *ex parte* notice by applicable local court rules, the company receives notification. If done on an *ex parte* basis, notice may be exceptionally short. In some extreme instances, the company receives no advance notice until after the receiver is appointed. In such cases, the party seeking to appoint the receiver must persuade the court that giving notice of the receivership will result in the dissipation of assets. The following illustrates an extreme case.

A consumer product distributor had a loan that was secured by the company's inventory and receivables, among other things. When the loan matured, the company advised its lender that the business had failed and had no receivables, cash, or inventory. The lender then, as would be customary, performed an investigation. What the lender found was substantial evidence of a successor company's operating the same business under a new name, with the same management team in place.

The appointed receiver found further disturbing evidence: the successor company was in the process of relocating millions of dollars of inventory to another state. After halting the activity, the receiver discovered transferred company inventory in three Midwestern states and Canada.

Subsequently, the receiver applied *ex parte*, and without notice, to four separate courts, seeking to have the California order appointing receiver recognized in each state and Canada. After reviewing evidence, the court granted relief and appointed the receiver in all four jurisdictions without notice to the company, based on the evidence of the improper conduct. The court appropriately acknowledged that, in this case, prior notice would have enabled the company to continue to attempt to secretly transfer the inventory to the other locations in violation of the order appointing the receiver. The court ruled that the successor company was nothing more than a new business carrying out the old company's affairs.

The receiver was then able to auction off all recovered inventory in three different states and Canada, obtaining millions of dollars for the secured lender's benefit. One company principal was eventually criminally charged and sentenced to prison. Another principal fled to China as a fugitive. Had the company been provided with advance notice of the receiver's extended appointment, the receiver's ability to recover assets would likely have been delayed or hindered.

What to Expect When a Receiver is Appointed

Upon appointment, the equity receiver must take quick action. First, the receiver and his or her team will go to the business to serve employees with the order appointing the receiver. Next, the receiver will secure computers, records, offices, websites, internet access, bank accounts, and credit card terminals and will swiftly take additional action, as necessary, to carry out the court-mandated duties. It is at this early stage of the receivership that the company's owner(s) and employee(s) have a crucial decision to make. Will they cooperate?

In the company's best interest, management and employees should cooperate with the receiver, whose duty is to act in a cost-effectively manner. Noncooperation will drive up costs for the company, as it must pay from its business assets all the fees accrued hourly by receivers and their attorneys, accountants, forensic consultants, and other professionals. However, since receivership is usually not a welcome alternative for management, it is not unusual for the company to resist the receiver's actions to limit it.

Furthermore, given the scope and authority of orders appointing receivers, if illicit activity is suspected or alleged, it is almost certain to be found if it exists. For example, in order to uncover the money trail of any disputed funds, the receiver will employ forensic accountants. That is what happened in the following case.

A certain company had some advance notice that a receiver was to be appointed in federal court after a U.S. governmental agency alleged that it was engaged in securities violations. Upon takeover, the receiver discovered that the company had deleted all emails from its server. Computer forensic consultants eventually found a hidden drawer containing the server's back up tapes and recovered hundreds of thousands of emails. The evidence was instrumental in assisting the receiver and his forensic accountants in reconstructing the activities of the fraudulent enterprise, which included over 8,000 investors from over 10 countries, who invested over $250 million with the company.

Of course, not every company that enters receivership engages in outright fraud. There may be other situations in which just one partner is engaged in deceptive conduct or is in violation of contracts or agreements, yet the underlying business is legitimate. In those cases, another partner might file a lawsuit against the illicit partner and subsequently seek appointment of a receiver to preserve the company, pending the outcome of the underlying litigation.

Sometimes in the early stages of receivership, the receiver does not want the company's customers and vendors to know of his or her existence, as it may be disruptive to the company's ability to continue as a going concern. An experienced receiver will always make every reasonable effort to operate the business behind the scenes by implementing a proper set of checks and balances. The receiver may remove company personnel as signers on bank accounts and begin to promote industry best practices, treat employees with respect and professionalism, and take other necessary steps to preserve and maintain the business.

Business Operations under Receivership

When a receiver initially takes over business operations, employees, especially non-principals, are typically concerned about how the receivership may impact their jobs. In some cases, however, assuming that the business will remain open and that the employees are performing adequately, the receiver can become a calming element in an otherwise chaotic setting, especially if principals are engaged in improper conduct, disputes, or legal maneuvering.

Because the receiver's job is to ensure that the company adheres to all applicable laws governing business operations, when specific unlawful, pre-receivership practices exist, the receiver will bring the company into compliance. Such actions may prove to benefit both employees and operations, at least in the long term.

The most common practices that the receiver will review and correct include

- *Compliance with wage/hour laws.* All state and federal wage/hour laws apply to receivership, including proper classification of employees versus independent contractors, overtime, payroll taxes, health insurance, COBRA, and workers' compensation insurance, and employees must be lawfully authorized to work in the U.S.

- *The timely filing of tax returns.* State and federal tax returns must be prepared and filed on time unless otherwise directed by the court. If a receiver operates a business, tax returns are not timely filed, and there are unpaid tax liabilities during the receivership period, a receiver may be held personally liable for the money due.

- *Payment of only legitimate company expenses.* If a company is paying the owners' or owners' family members' personal expenses and fails to report those payments properly, the receivership estate will end this practice.

- *Stoppage of unreported cash payments.* Service industry businesses, such as restaurants, often pay employees in cash. A receiver may not compensate employees or independent contractors in cash and must withhold all applicable taxes and report all wages.

Adhering strictly to lawful practices often increases operating costs for companies, along with a corresponding decrease in net operating income. While this may create conflicts between the receiver and company owners, the receiver is an agent of the court with an obligation to operate companies properly, regardless of the financial impact. If lawful operation creates an insolvency situation, then the receiver must consider whether or not the company can continue to operate as a going concern.

The Forensic Accountant

Forensic accounting provides a money trail that the receiver will follow. Using a forensic accountant in receivership is quite common. To the extent that the company failed to maintain its books and records properly, the receiver, along with other professionals such as a forensic accountant, can probably reconstruct its records and restate tax returns if necessary. But this process can be very lengthy and costly, depending on the level of cooperation or interference by the company.

For example, the receiver may determine from the forensic accountant's report that there were fraudulent or other recoverable transfers at the onset of a company's financial distress. These would include company transactions used to hinder, delay, or defraud creditors; when a reasonably equivalent value was absent from a transaction; or when some form of insolvency existed at the time of transfer. Likewise, when company assets have been transferred or sold to avoid the jurisdiction of the receiver or creditors, the receiver has the legal authority to seek recovery of those assets.

A case in point involved a receiver in a judgment enforcement action against a tax preparation firm with multiple locations in southern California. When the receiver arrived to take possession of the tax preparation firm, the owner advised him that all its offices in various cities had been sold and were no longer assets encumbered by the judgment. After numerous emergency court hearings, the court ruled that the company's sale was, in fact, done to avoid collection by the judgment creditor. The receiver was then ordered to take possession of all assets of the successor company, which triggered the judgment debtor to request an immediate settlement because the receiver was planning on taking over all locations immediately before tax season. The case was settled shortly after that, with the judgment creditor receiving approximately 80 percent of the judgment's face value.

Other Receiverships

Judgment Enforcement Receivership. In the domain of lawsuits over debts, a judgment is the equivalent of a judge's stamp of approval that someone owes someone else money. For the creditor who initiated the lawsuit and obtained the judgment against the debtor, it can be an empty victory if there is no realistic chance of collecting on it, as a judgment represents only the debtor's obligation to pay; it does not guarantee payment. If the debtor does not satisfy the judgment voluntarily, the creditor will resort to various tactics to collect on the debt. One of those tactics may be to initiate a legal action requesting the appointment of a "judgment enforcement receiver" to aid in the recovery of the judgment. In most cases, the judgment enforcement receiver will have the court's authority to take full possession over the company assets owned by the debtor under judgment and to determine whether the company is viable as a going concern, and if so, whether it is profitable. Unlike the pre-judgment receiver, the judgment enforcement receiver works directly for the benefit of the judgment creditor.

Judgment enforcement receiverships usually take one of two primary approaches. In the first approach, if the company is profitable, the receiver will likely continue to operate the company, retain key personnel, if they can be trusted, and impose new checks and balances. Like other pre-judgment receiverships, this can include taking sole control over all bank accounts and exerting control over income and expenses. Ultimately, the receiver's goal is to operate the company with as little interference as possible, keep operational debts paid, and sweep excess cash into the receiver's trust account on a periodic basis until adequate funds are recovered to satisfy the judgment and to pay the receiver's fees and expenses. The judgment receiver must also verify that there are no other senior lienholders (such as taxing agencies) before disbursing funds to the judgment creditor or creditors. The receiver will also institute a claim procedure whereby creditors have an opportunity to assert claims against the receivership estate. The receiver must ensure that subordinate creditors are not paid prior to senior secured creditors, and if the receiver fails to establish and abide by a proper procedure, it may result in personal liability.

The second type of judgment enforcement receivership scenario is very drastic. When the receiver determines that the company is not viable as a going concern, the receiver will liquidate all company assets and pay all creditors, in the order of priority required by state law, as the company winds down. In some instances, a receiver may find a buyer for the entire business or auction company assets to the highest bidder.

Divorce Receivership. A receiver may be appointed in marital dissolution actions if matrimonial assets appear to be in danger of being dissipated, or if one spouse is refusing to provide material financial information to the other. A receiver can also be empowered to enforce spousal support and attorneys' fees orders. Typically, one party will seek to have a receiver appointed to take control over such assets, and the judge administering the divorce proceeding will appoint that receiver. The receiver may employ forensic accountants and take all necessary action to preserve and maintain the marital assets.

The receiver who is appointed over a company in a divorce case will operate, preserve, and maintain the company pending further order of the court. The receiver will typically seek to shield the company's customers from the details of the receivership to preserve the company's reputation. A receiver in a divorce action may also be empowered to liquidate all company assets under court order via a public auction, depending on circumstances.

To see how this works, let's look at the case of a Los Angeles company under receivership during the owner's divorce process. The owner/husband had developed a severe drug dependency, was showing up at the business under the influence of drugs, acting erratically, and was eventually banned from the building by the building owner. The receiver was appointed shortly after that, only to find that many employees were on the verge of resigning, payroll taxes were unpaid, workers' compensation insurance was unpaid, and the company was under eviction for nonpayment of rent. Other payables were piling up.

The receiver was able to restore confidence among the staff and discussed the situation with the landlord, effectuating a payment plan for rent and saving the business from being evicted. The receiver also worked out a payment plan with taxing agencies regarding past-due taxes and rehabilitated the company's image with clients. The divorce was final, with the business's being bought by the owner's ex-wife.

Government Enforcement Receivership. The U.S. Securities & Exchange Commission and the Federal Trade Commission regularly seek the appointment of receivers in cases involving securities and consumer fraud, respectively. Securities fraud cases often involve Ponzi-like schemes wherein funds from new investors are used to pay returns to previous investors because funds from company operations are either insufficient or nonexistent due to outright fraud. Consumer fraud cases involve products and/or services offered to the public in a deceitful or fraudulent manner. In both instances, the appointed receiver immediately seeks to determine whether the allegations of the government agency are accurate and if so, the operations of the company will likely cease.

Government enforcement actions typically involve parallel criminal investigations, wherein the FBI and U.S. Department of Justice may review records and seek evidence. The appointment of a receiver triggers a notice to owners, employees, and customers. The receiver's goal is to ultimately recover assets for defrauded investors and consumers, which in most cases means that the company is shut down and all assets liquidated.

The bar is set very high to have a receiver appointed in these types of cases. If the court appoints a receiver, the evidence considered by the court is usually overwhelming, as the court must also determine the degree of public harm if the drastic remedy of appointing a receiver is not employed.

Filing Bankruptcy in Response to Receiverships

The filing of a bankruptcy results in an automatic stay which precludes any creditor from taking action against the company. One such stay action is the appointment of a receiver. Accordingly, if it appears that a receiver may be appointed, it is not usual for management to preempt that appointment by the filing of a bankruptcy. While the filing of the bankruptcy may preclude a receiver's appointment, if the company has engaged in outright fraud, then the bankruptcy court may appoint a trustee in the bankruptcy case itself.

If, on the other hand, a receiver has already been appointed, the filing of bankruptcy after that will not preclude the appointment of a receiver. However, the bankruptcy laws do require that if a business is in the hands of a receiver, then the receiver must turn that business back to management upon the filing of a bankruptcy. Even in this case, however, the party who sought appointment of the receiver may petition the bankruptcy court to waive the "turnover" requirement to allow the receiver to stay in possession. The bankruptcy court will consider such a request on a case-by-case basis.

Receivership Termination

The facts and circumstances surrounding receiverships will determine when a court eventually will terminate the receiver. In some cases, the court will return the company and its assets to the owner. In other cases, the company will have been restructured, sold, or liquidated.

Receivership is a valuable and powerful tool that can be used by the government or parties seeking satisfaction on judgments or protections/remedies related to the improper acts of business partners or spouses. While the appointment of a receiver does not automatically mean that the company will cease to operate, understanding the powers, duties, and obligations of the court-appointed receiver will assist in determining how best to comply with all applicable court orders.

— ◇ —

Stephen J. Donell, CPM, ARM, CCIM, is president of FedReceiver, Inc., based in Los Angeles. Since 1990, Mr. Donell has administered and/or been appointed as a receiver in more than 600 cases in state and federal courts in receivership matters involving residential and commercial real estate and business operations and liquidations. He also has administered and/or been appointed as receiver in actions filed by the United States Securities and Exchange Commission, the Federal Trade Commission, and other government enforcement actions involving business fraud. In 2013 he completed his third consecutive year as the co-president of the Los Angeles/Orange County chapter of the California Receivers Forum (CRF) and is a past president of the National Association of Federal Equity Receivers (NAFER). Contact him at Steve.Donell@fedreceiver.com.

www.ingramcontent.com/pod-product-compliance
Lightning Source LLC
Chambersburg PA
CBHW031808190326
41518CB00006B/247